There's Only One

Jockey International

In loving memory of Donna Wolf Steigerwaldt

Chairman of the Board and Chief Executive Officer

1929-2000

There's Only One

Jockey International

Jay Pridmore

GREENWICH PUBLISHING GROUP, INC.
LYME, CONNECTICUT

Produced and published by Greenwich Publishing Group, Inc.
Lyme, Connecticut

Design by Clare Cunningham Graphic Design

Library of Congress Card Number: 2001091275

ISBN: 0-944641-49-0

First Printing: June 2001

10 9 8 7 6 5 4 3 2 1

Photography Credits:
Pages 6, 10 and 11 appear courtesy of Fort Miami Heritage Society, page 47 appears courtesy of *Kenosha News*.

All other images appear courtesy of Jockey International, Inc.

About the Author:
Jay Pridmore is a journalist and author whose books include histories of Northwestern University (2000) and The Museum of Science and Industry (1996), among other books about the history of Chicago and the Midwest. His books for Greenwich Publishing include *A Century of Success: The AmerUs Life Story* (1996) and *The Richardson Story: A Family Enterprise at 150 Years* (1998). He is also the author of *Chicago Architecture and Design* (1993) and *The American Bicycle* (1995).

Table of Contents

Cooper, Wells & Company was the pride of St. Joseph, Michigan, and did everything in the hosiery trade from spinning and knitting to advertising and selling. In the 1880s, the firm had a workforce of more than 100. In the 1890s, the Cooper side of the business moved to Wisconsin, where the company that would become Jockey International quickly grew and soon flourished.

Pioneer Origins

INDUSTRIAL
Spinning & Knitting
WORKS,
COOPER, WELLS & CO., *Proprietors*,
—MANUFACTURERS OF—
COTTON and WOOLEN SOCKS.
Boys and girls can find employment by applying at the factory
Foot of Broad Street, St. Joseph, Mich.

The company that would become Jockey International was founded not far from the American frontier in 1876. It was born with enduring and ironclad strengths, many of which came from its founder, the Reverend Samuel Cooper, who exemplified the soaring spirit and inventiveness of the people who settled the land as pioneers.

Samuel Thrall Cooper, born in Ohio in 1824, made a career in the Midwest when the region was little more than wilderness and among people who built their towns and livelihoods from the ground up — and faced their sometimes bleak circumstances with optimism.

By middle age, Cooper was not only successful in manufacturing and trade, he also had a career in something just as basic to his time and place, the ministry. Preaching the word of God was a popular profession for bright young men on the frontier, but it was by no means an easy life. The work of an itinerant preacher meant travel, ministering

The Reverend Samuel Thrall Cooper, above, was the founder and inspirational leader of the company. His skill as a salesman made Cooper Wells a name synonymous with quality materials and craftsmanship. Willis W. Cooper, opposite, Samuel's oldest son, possessed the management skills that transformed the family business into a large operation with ready capital, industrial machines and widespread sales.

to the widely dispersed faithful, and all-too-frequent encounters with the godless. It meant leaving one's family for long periods of time, all of which came with honor but little in the way of remuneration.

Reverend Cooper's only possible motivation for such work was a sincere devotion to the spiritual welfare of others, a quality that he displayed all his life. While he had taken no vow of poverty — nor was his Methodist Church resistant to the accumulation of worldly wealth — his impulse to serve was unshakably strong. When he later moved into business as a way to better support his family, Cooper's sense of the common good kept him in church work and remained an underpinning of his conduct.

A sense of fairness and decency ran deep in Cooper's character and in that of his family. Samuel's father before him, also named Samuel, was a Methodist preacher as well, who came to his calling after years of a hard life as a pioneer in Ohio, Indiana and Illinois. The senior Cooper was "converted to God after a season of deep repentance and sorrow for sin," as it was later described in a short biography in a Methodist publication. He was licensed to exhort as a circuit-riding minister who traveled long distances, "preaching his great salvation to perishing sinners."

Riding the Circuit

Young Samuel initially was not encouraged to follow his father into the preaching life. His parents envisioned him in a trade and placed him as an apprentice with a tanner in Lafayette, Indiana. But tanning was swiftly eclipsed by a religious awakening that Samuel

experienced as an adolescent. His impulse to serve only grew in succeeding years. By the age of 21, the future founder of Jockey International had started his fruitful career with the Methodist Church.

Samuel's life as frontier preacher was not too different from that of his father. He would ride hundreds of miles each week, preaching nearly every day — often in unsavory outposts where the word of the Lord held little sway. Also like his father, he was transferred to a succession of districts, mostly in Indiana, where he preached, baptized and attended to institutional work — he was long active on the board of Asbury Methodist College, later DePauw University.

It was while riding the church circuit around Michigan City, Indiana, that Samuel Cooper met his future wife, Mary Ward, whose family had come west a few years before from Utica, New York. Samuel and Mary were married in 1851, and the couple proceeded to have and raise six children. While Samuel's career as a churchman continued to grow, his vocation competed vigorously with family responsibilities, in terms of the time that it took him away from home and the material support that his family needed but his salary did not provide.

Such hardships were aggravated in 1868, when Samuel was thrown from a buggy while traveling on behalf of the church and was seriously injured. The reverend took only a few months off, but his leg did not heal as hoped. Thus, after much prayer, Samuel requested and was granted a "supernumerary position" with the church, a semi-retired status that allowed Cooper a more reasonable schedule and time for work more suitable to a family man.

He was never one to sit and watch grass grow, however. Samuel soon took a position as a traveling salesman for a manufacturer of school furniture, A. H. Andrews Company of Chicago. Whether or not this provided the desired income, it continued to keep him away from his family, which was hardly ideal. There is even an account that when the family home burned during this period, Samuel was unaware of the tragedy until he returned a week later.

Also around this time, the Coopers' eldest son, Willis, who was 17 years old in 1871, struck out on his own. Willis moved to St. Joseph, Michigan, where he accepted a position with the Wells Basket Company, a fortunate choice primarily because of the character of his employer, Abel W. Wells. Wells, also a Methodist of high standing in the church, had built a thriving business that served the growers of strawberries, blueberries, cranberries, cherries and other varieties of fruit widely cultivated in southwest Michigan. In many ways, he was an astute man of commerce who discerned that Willis Cooper had potential, and he quickly gave the young man a management position and an opportunity to acquire stock in the company.

The Preacher in Business

It is likely that Abel Wells's successful example inspired the entrepreneurial urge in Samuel Cooper. In 1875 or 1876, the reverend moved the rest of his family to live near Willis in St. Joseph. The elder Cooper had accumulated a little capital that he believed was

sufficient to go into business for himself. Thus he was receptive, perhaps overly so, when introduced to a man eager to sell six knitting machines — well adapted, Cooper was told, to the manufacture of hosiery.

Samuel Cooper liked the idea of manufacturing hosiery. He rightly noted that store-bought clothing was on the rise throughout the nation — partly because of the expansion of garment manufacturing by ex-military suppliers after the Civil War. Cooper understood, furthermore, that wool production in Michigan was on the rise, and he was also confident that his salesmanship cultivated as a minister could serve to capture a market for goods of high quality. Thus in 1876 he founded S. T. Cooper and Sons, so named because it would also involve sons Willis, Henry and eventually Charles, who was still a child.

While Cooper's concept was sound, there were problems in the execution. What the reverend had not recognized initially, for one, was that the knitting equipment he had purchased from the "oily, smooth talker," as one of the Cooper sons later described the seller, was anything but state-of-the-art. Each required the full-time attentions of an employee and was far slower than the automated systems of many other plants in the 1870s.

But Cooper stayed the course that he had chosen, which was to turn out goods of the highest quality possible. He also embarked on a modernization strategy to overcome his unfortunate start and frankly sorry equipment. Within two years, the company had industrial knitting machines, boilers and engines to run them, a dye house, a yarn-spinning operation and a modest brick building to house them all. By 1879, with additional investment from Abel Wells, and, renamed Cooper, Wells & Company, the business was engaged in buying local wool, spinning it, knitting it, and manufacturing a line of hosiery for men, women and children. The mill was also called Industrial Spinning and Knitting Works to reflect its larger size and scope. It employed some 90 employees, mostly women, who operated the machines that turned out 200 dozen pairs of seamless stockings per day.

Hard Work and Goodwill

Business was not without its stresses, of course, as payments on new equipment came due well before profits were sufficient to pay them. While this reality fairly terrorized his family, Reverend Cooper remained unflappable

In 1879, Cooper, Wells & Co. expanded with this new factory, above, called "mammoth" by the local newspaper at the time. As seen at right, inside the factory were steam-powered knitting machines and other equipment that produced 200 dozen pairs of wool and cotton stockings per day. This figure increased steadily as markets grew and manufacturing techniques improved.

in the face of these obligations. "My father once told me that because he made it a rule to pay his bills promptly," Henry Cooper wrote years later, "he had won the reputation of being a man of property; whereas, his financial strength was greatly over-rated." The illusion turned out to be an asset. "Due to my father's reputation for integrity," wrote Henry, "we were able to get extensions on our debts, enabling us to pay them off after a time."

These were the beginnings of a family business whose name was synonymous with hard work and honest dealing. And no matter what the nature of Cooper finances in these years, Samuel's reputation for a generous community spirit was undisputed. No matter how busy he was at the mill, he always made time to serve as guest minister in Methodist pulpits throughout southwest Michigan. In this, he "won the hearts of all by his earnest devotion to the cause of Christ and by his frank, genial disposition," as recorded by the newspaper in the town of Three Oaks, where he took to the pulpit on several occasions.

Cooper emerged as a valued member of the economic community as well. Within a year of his arriving in the area, for example, he was elected vice president of the St. Joseph Improvement Association. With Abel Wells as president, the association was deeply involved in attracting new industry to St. Joseph, an important port city on Lake Michigan whose dominance was being threatened by new railroads. As St. Joe's biggest boosters, Cooper and Wells had several successes in attracting industry to the town. Cooper's own business leapt forward after a large knitting mill in

Henry S. Cooper, top, brought the company great prosperity and national recognition. His younger brother Charles F. Cooper, above, grew up in the business.

nearby Niles burned down, Cooper made sure that this tragedy's silver lining would be good for St. Joseph and good for Samuel Cooper as well.

He formed a plan to rehire the skilled mill workers to an expanded Cooper factory at St. Joseph. It was a logical idea that lacked only the necessary capital, which Abel Wells invested. The factory's success was also due in large part to the arrival of J. W. Hart, ex-superintendent at Niles — all of which helped make Cooper, Wells & Co. one of the largest knitting manufacturers in Michigan. "Our citizens begin to realize," wrote a local newspaper, "what may be done for their town by a liberal and united effort."

An Uncommon Enterprise

Among many ingredients for the success of this mill were the Cooper sons, who were key managers in the family business and, by the 1880s, major stockholders. Willis had been the central figure in establishing the original mill and organizing all aspects of subsequent expansions. Second son Henry was likewise well-rounded, beginning his career in the office and later working in manufacturing. Charles, the youngest boy, was too young for work when the mill was founded but already showed signs that he would contribute at an early age.

Samuel Cooper's métier, meanwhile, was sales. His talents as a minister, plus the luxury of having sons who could run the business, enabled the reverend to spend his time doing what he did best: riding the circuit, talking to customers and preaching the indisputable advantages of Cooper Wells quality.

For the manufacturer to sell directly to the retailer was uncommon at this time in the knit-goods business. The usual method was to ship the entire stock to commissioned brokers, who in turn sold to the stores. But Cooper never liked brokers, he said, because they left the manufacturer too little control over volume and price. What he didn't say was that he was addicted to travel; not long after the family got into the hosiery business, Reverend Cooper became one of the first salesmen in the business to work directly for the factory, and he expanded business with accounts as far west as Seattle, Washington.

The company moved ahead, sometimes by chance but always with a sharp eye for new markets. One significant new market turned up in the north woods of Minnesota, where Abel Wells had once worked in the lumber business. Wells knew many lumberjacks and learned that they not only valued good woolen stockings, but had trouble finding anything not made with common "shoddy," or the floor sweepings of knitting mills. Many of them got good socks from local women, who knitted them by hand. Thus, Wells convinced Cooper to pay a visit to the north woods himself. It wasn't long before lumbermen would wear no other brand of socks but Cooper Wells, proving what Samuel Cooper believed all along; there's always a niche to be filled, and that niche is yours if you fill it with quality goods.

Cooper Wells's success in lumber country was not the only example of the company's steady progress. Another success story developed out of a failure, after the company purchased a new-fangled stitching machine designed to sew shut the toes of knit stockings with cotton thread. Unfortunately the technique did not outperform the old method, which was to finish the hosiery by hand, and was abandoned. While the machine was quickly discarded out of sight, the large stock of strong, soft cotton thread was left in the warehouse, where it never failed to irritate Henry Cooper every time he walked past. In part to relieve his aggravation, Henry used the thread for a new model of boys' knee stockings, which turned out to be popular and were given a name that was associated with Cooper Wells for years: Iron Clad.

The Death of Reverend Cooper

Reverend Cooper's spiritual and social gifts were many, and when he passed away in 1892 at the age of 68, it was a great shock to the people of St. Joseph and beyond. Reports of his death stated that he had complained of few ailments in his final months. When he collapsed and died of apoplexy in his home, "the call was so sudden that few could realize that the aged preacher and citizen had gone — his pleasant voice, his familiar figure would be heard and seen no more with us on earth," wrote the *St. Joseph Herald*.

Certainly, the death of their father moved the Cooper brothers in profound ways. It also triggered an independent streak in all three of them, who inherited the reverend's shares in the knitting business, sold them (mostly to Wells) and left the partnership. It was reported that there were policy differences between the brothers and Abel Wells, though they were anything but bitter, judging from the Coopers' fond memories for their father's former partner in later years. It may be that Wells was ready to take a more active role in the business; in the next decade he more than doubled the size of the operation, and Cooper, Wells & Co. continued in the hosiery business into the 1950s. Or it could be that the Coopers simply needed new challenges, which they found.

Henry Cooper moved to Midland, Michigan, to work for the Dow Chemical Company. Willis and Charles remained in the line they knew best and took positions with the Chicago-Rockford Hosiery Company in Illinois. This move was evidently influenced by J. W. Hart, former factory manager at Cooper Wells; in fact, Chicago-Rockford turned out to be a custom-made opportunity for ambitious young men. The company was expanding and preparing to move to a new and larger mill in Kenosha, Wisconsin. They needed experienced management, in return for which current stockholders were offering a share in the ownership.

The situation was a happy one for several years. Chicago-Rockford did grow, the Coopers did acquire significant stock and before long, the company even had room for their brother Henry, who joined in 1900. Indeed, as Chicago-Rockford Hosiery moved to Kenosha, Wisconsin, and renamed itself Chicago-Kenosha, its potential as the Cooper family's next business seemed very promising indeed. Through tenacity and concentration, the promise would soon become a reality, and the company prospered, though in a different form from what the brothers had imagined when they moved with their families to Wisconsin.

On Prairie Avenue (later 60th Street) the Chicago-Kenosha Hosiery Company, maker of Black Cat hosiery, became a major firm in wool and cotton hosiery. Willis Cooper invested his expertise and his assets in this operation in 1892, and a few years later started an underwear operation in unused mill space. This view of the factory would change in 1900, when Cooper and his brother Charles incorporated the Cooper Underwear Company and began construction of a separate mill on an adjacent site.

The Move

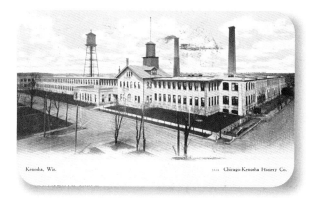

Kenosha, Wis.   Chicago-Kenosha Hosiery Co.

When Willis Cooper traveled to Kenosha in 1892, the city wasn't much to look at. Paved streets were a new development, and while convenient, they were imperfect, collapsing from time to time and swallowing horses and wagons in a single gulp. Kenosha had romantic origins, named after the Indian word for game fish that were once plentiful in the area. But it was now a railroad town, and the railroads had done a better job at bringing vagrants and grit than anything like storybook prosperity.

Things were looking up, however. By 1890, a new jail kept tramps off the street, and Kenosha's Simmon's Mattress Company, the world's largest maker of beds and mattresses, was 20 years old. While the jail was an important accommodation, the importance of a major industry to the small Wisconsin town can hardly be overstated. The Simmons Company had over 900 employees by the time the Coopers moved to Kenosha, and its founder, Zalmon G. Simmons, was Kenosha's most influential citizen. Past mayor, public financier and capitalist of international renown, Simmons had made his first fortune in dry goods, his second in cheese boxes and his third in telegraphy; only later did he get into beds. He was known for the nostrum: "The busy dollar alone earns a profit."

Simmons was a particular inspiration for Kenosha businessmen who were making more modest fortunes in other enterprises — wagon shops, furniture manufacturing, leather tanneries and brass foundries — and were busy looking for opportunities to multiply their newly earned dollars. By the early 1890s, one such likely venture emerged in the Chicago-Rockford Hosiery Company, formerly located in Rockford, Illinois, but now looking to relocate closer to the burgeoning markets of Chicago and Milwaukee.

Thus did several investors from Kenosha, including executives from the Bain Wagon Works and American Brass, put their money behind the idea of bringing knitting to their city. The plan was to build a new mill a mile west of downtown, seek competent management and watch what they hoped would be the West's next hosiery empire flourish and grow.

Black Cat of Kenosha

Willis Cooper arrived in Kenosha in 1892 with contacts, knowledge and unfettered ambition. He had been lured to Wisconsin by J. W. Hart, former superintendent of Cooper Wells who had become president of Chicago-Rockford. As Willis joined the management team, he made it clear that he was a good match for a growing company.

Willis quickly made his mark on Chicago-Rockford and in 1895 was made general manager with broad influence over manufacturing and sales. He also acquired an ownership share, which he was determined to see grow. It was an agreeable situation that enabled Willis do what he probably had planned all

Kenosha, Wisconsin, seen above in 1887, was a fine home for the Coopers. Charles's children, Ralph and Carlotta Cooper, at play beside the Black Cat factory in the photo at right, would have major roles in the company. Black Cat advertisements, opposite page, ran in national publications such as the *Ladies' Home Journal*, and the importance of national advertising was a lesson that the Coopers took to heart.

along, which was to bring his family into the company as well. First, he installed his younger brother Charles, who had grown up around spinning and knitting, as general superintendent in the plant. Then Willis concentrated on what had made Cooper Wells a force in its own right: a sales network along the lines of the one his father had built some two decades before.

Within just a few years, Willis had two dozen salesmen on the road, covering the Midwest and a good part of the West as well. The sales force was energetic and enthusiastic about reminding retailers of the benefits of first-quality hosiery. For the entire line, the best-quality cotton and long-fiber wool were used. Knee stockings for boys, a good seller here as they had been for Cooper Wells, boasted double stitching at the knee and twice the durability of the competition. Within two years, the company adopted the trade name "Black Cat," which became recognized across the country as first-class hosiery for men, women and children.

White Cat Underwear

As Willis and Charles Cooper acquired an increasing financial share of the business, they moved it in an ambitious new direction: underwear. While men's underwear was a knitted product, like stockings, that was where similarity ended. Underwear was entirely more complex to manufacture, requiring larger knitting equipment to start and new sewing machines to finish, along with trained employees to operate them. This was not a simple sideline, and some Chicago-Rockford (now renamed Chicago-Kenosha)

They Outwear Two Pairs of Ordinary Stockings

Black Cat
Reinforced Hosiery

For Correct Attire

SUBSTANTIAL citizens of OUR TOWN believe in wearing the best. That is why you see so many with Black Cat Hose; distinguishable by even, well-woven surface; snug, elastic fit; clear, permanent dyes.

Black Cat provides for both sexes of all ages. It protects the infant's toddling steps—sees boys and girls through the play period, and for grown-ups comes in sheer, pure silk, fine of weave, comfortable and correct.

Back of the style and beauty of Black Cat Hosiery is always the watchword *DURABILITY*—the reinforcements of heel, sole, toe and top that give long life and lasting satisfaction.

Dealers who buy and sell on a basis of *VALUE* carry a full line of Black Cat Hosiery for men, women and children.

BLACK CAT TEXTILES COMPANY, *Kenosha, Wisconsin*
Cooper's-Bennington Spring Needle Underwear for Men
Is Made and Marketed by Black Cat Textiles Company

From original drawing by W. B. King

In the beginning, Black Cat hosiery was for lumberjacks and others with a serious need for durable socks. But the brand soon expanded to include hosiery "for men, women and children" that was billed as "correct attire," left. The Cooper brothers built on the popularity of the Black Cat brand when they went into business manufacturing union suits under the brand name "White Cat," above.

partners opposed the idea. Still, Charles and Willis prevailed, confident that it was an opportunity to grab hold of. Black Cat hosiery salesmen were soon selling underwear as well, and while this seems like an obvious move today, the Coopers' "make-what-we-sell" philosophy was relatively new at that time, when a company's manufacturing people usually dictated what its sales force had to sell.

Another reason for getting into the underwear business was less obvious. Men's underwear was in a moment of transition, and the union suit was the new fashion at the time. So-called because it "unified" the top and bottom, the union suit was invented in the early 1890s by textile manufacturer George D. Munsing as a sleeker and more comfortable alternative to the baggy, bulking undergarments of old. While the brothers remained active with Black Cat hosiery, they also rented excess space in the hosiery mill to manufacture what they branded "White Cat" underwear.

The new line did better than most expected, and it wasn't long before the Coopers induced other investors to help them expand in union suits. Chief among them was their third brother, Henry, who left his job at Dow Chemical in Michigan

The tag line "Big Enough and Long Enough" described the comfort of White Cat undergarments. And the management of the Cooper Underwear Company believed that behind comfortable underwear were happy seamstresses, which they appear to have had.

to join the new family business in Kenosha. New capital and management talent led to a new spurt of growth for White Cat, which featured woolen union suits for winter use and cotton ones for summer. These were the beginning of a richly varied product line that from this time on would characterize the underwear turned out by this family. In 1900, the brothers incorporated their enterprise, calling it, prosaically enough, the Cooper Underwear Company. The company was incorporated with capital of $150,000, and work on a separate mill was begun adjacent to the Black Cat mill. The White Cat mill on Prairie Avenue (later 60th Street) went up on the site of what later became the headquarters of Jockey International.

Whatever else the Coopers manufactured in this period, they certainly generated the goodwill that became a major key to their success. They also avoided their natural inclination to become workaholics. All were active in the local Methodist Church and involved themselves in the wider affairs of the town as well. They were organizers of Kenosha's first YMCA. Willis also used his verbal and sales skills, a gift from his father, as leader of the statewide Prohibition Party and its candidate for lieutenant governor.

Such a straightforward community spirit was tied to everything the brothers did, including their business, where it translated into quality on every level. "It is easier to do a thing right than to do it wrong," Abel Wells always told the Cooper boys when they were together in St. Joseph. Now on their own, the Coopers adopted Wells's blunt but indisputable philosophy and even expanded upon it, again with a touch more eloquence as time passed. Henry Cooper, in his long life, coined aphorisms of his own such as, "Our prices are subject to change without notice, but our quality never varies."

Such verities translated into underwear that became known in stores throughout the nation for certain attributes that were absent in competitive product. Cooper Underwear Co. preshrunk the fabric, for example, a "little matter," said Henry, that "runs into many thousands of dollars which are spent simply for the comfort and satisfaction of the ultimate consumer." Happily, the Cooper brothers

understood that while most American men didn't talk about their underwear, they knew the difference quality made to their everyday comfort. The Coopers were extraordinary for many reasons, but among them was their ability to articulate a commitment to the comfort and fit of high-quality men's nether garments, while most of the competition could promote little else beyond price.

Trial and Triumph

Sales quickly proved that the Coopers' message was on the mark. Business grew to $183,000 in sales in 1903. Profits on these sales were very good as well — almost $37,000 that same year — and the conscientious Coopers were only too happy to plow these earnings back into the business, as the company consistently did in the years that followed.

While the public was hearing the Coopers' mantra-like promise of quality and fit, the company was also listening to the customers; and in listening, the company was quick to focus its attention on an unsolved problem with the union suit. This problem, as everyone knew, was the trap door bottom —

Chicago-Kenosha Hosiery Co.
Manufacturers of Seamless and Full Fashioned Hosiery

BLACK CAT BRAND — *We warrant every pair of Stockings bearing this brand*

Kenosha, Wis., U. S. A. /19/05.

SOLD TO _____ Mr. J. D. Byrne,

NO. 290   AGENT   J F G   VIA   M. P.   Pirds Point, Mo.-

TERMS: NET 30 DAYS, OR 2 PER CENT 10 DAYS.   Nov. 15th.

NOTICE:— ALL CLAIMS FOR ERRORS OR SHORTAGE MUST BE MADE WITHIN FIVE DAYS AFTER RECEIPT OF GOODS.

NO. OF DOZ.	STYLE	DESCRIPTION	PRICE	TOTAL	
12	14	Childrens Hose	92	11 04	
3	600	Ladies Hose	2 25	6 75	
3	16	Ladies Hose	2 15	6 45	
3	116	Ladies Hose	2 25	6 75	
20	172	Gents Socks	1 00	20 00	
5	173	Gents Socks	1 00	5 00	
5	142	Gents Socks	1 00	5 00	
5	143	Gents Socks	1 00	5 00	
20	77	Gents Socks	80	16 00	
10	3031	Gents Socks	2 00	20 00	
5	920	Gents Socks	2 25	11 25	$113.24

Terms as _____ Nov. 15th.
2 per cent 10 or net 30 days.

71

In remitting, please send New York or Chicago Exchange

The Cooper brothers knew they had a built-in network of dozens of salesmen who were traveling the Midwest and beyond selling Black Cat hosiery. Wherever Black Cat was sold, so followed White Cat underwear.

the drop seat that bunched and bulked in the best of times and, in the worst, jabbed the wearer with hard and inconveniently placed buttons. Until these design defects were corrected, union suits were, plain and simple, rubbing many American men the wrong way.

The Cooper Underwear Company would eventually produce the union suit of America's dreams, but not before the company and the family overcame a tragedy that overshadowed any commercial success they had enjoyed thus far. In late 1903, Willis and Charles Cooper were on a selling trip in Chicago. A few days after Christmas, the brothers decided to take a well-deserved afternoon off to see comedian Eddie Foy in a stage production of *Mr. Bluebeard* at the Iroquois Theater. In the second act of the play, a fire broke out in the theater, spreading so quickly that within 15 minutes, 600 of the 1,700 people in the theater were asphyxiated or crushed. The Iroquois Theater fire was one of the worst of its era, and among those who died were the Cooper brothers. When news of the tragedy reached Kenosha, Henry Cooper was left with two additional families and a business to take care of by himself. That he succeeded is a credit not only to him but also to the bonds that tied the family together.

Birth of an Idea

In the 20 years that Henry Cooper remained active in the business, he made many wise decisions. Perhaps the wisest was encouraging his plant superintendent, Horace Greeley Johnson, to keep thinking about the ideal union suit. Innovation was not yet the keynote of the apparel industry, but it was for Henry Cooper. This approach paid off handsomely in 1909, when Johnson finally came up with the breakthrough product.

White Cat's state-of-the-art union suit came to Johnson "almost like a dream," the inventor said, in the middle of the night. The story is that when it did, he got up and roused his wife, who stumbled over to the family sewing machine. With Johnson drawing on scraps of paper, his wife fabricated the first prototype of the union suit that became the ultimate in underwear — the "closed crotch."

The innovation was simple and ingenious. Instead of the drooping drop seat, the closed crotch was constructed as two pieces of fabric extending from front to back, one lapping over the other like an X. The pieces were held shut during normal wear by an unbreakable rubber button high on the haunch. But even without unbuttoning, the two sides could be easily drawn apart when the occasion demanded. Most importantly, the design had just one layer of fabric in the groin and buttock area, where the suit was most likely to bunch.

Though tedious to describe, the closed crotch was a delight to wear. When the Cooper Underwear sales force demonstrated the design to retailers — and retailers demonstrated it to customers — the union suit that became known as the Kenosha Klosed Krotch began its generation-long dominance of the national underwear industry.

The Kenosha Klosed Krotch union suit, invented in 1909, was the single greatest advance in underwear at that time. This sleek and convenient product jumped out of the backroom, where underclothes had been treated as a commodity, and into fine packaging in the front of the store.

Cooper Underwear demanded advertising that mirrored the quality and distinctiveness of the product. Here, in one of many fine paintings created by artist Joseph Leyendecker, the eye is drawn to men whose story illustrates the not-so-subtle difference between an ill-fitting union suit and a Kenosha Klosed Krotch model.

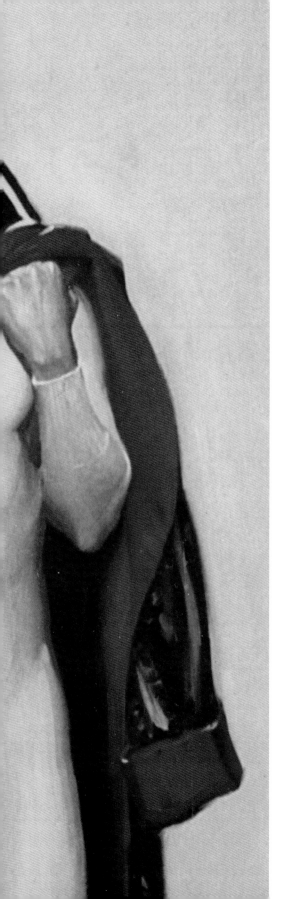

A More Perfect Union Suit

From the time it patented the Kenosha Klosed Krotch, the Cooper Underwear Company dominated its industry. The innovative union suit rose to the top of the underwear market so quickly and so convincingly that the company sold all the union suits it could make and licensed others to meet the seemingly endless demand. Horace Johnson, who shared the patent with Henry Cooper, became known as "Klosed Krotch" Johnson, as much for his legal work against infringers as for his inventing it in the first place. For Henry Cooper, the success of the Kenosha Klosed Krotch proved what he believed all

along — that a quality product and wide-awake salesmen made a combination of great power.

Savvy Salesmanship

Indeed, Henry Cooper maintained close contact with his sales force, pushing them to sell the Klosed Krotch as a "right and honest product," as was written in sales literature. These words were not invented by a hired copywriter from Chicago, rather they were part of Cooper's own torrent of inspirational slogans that the owner penned himself and transmitted to the field. "Opportunity is

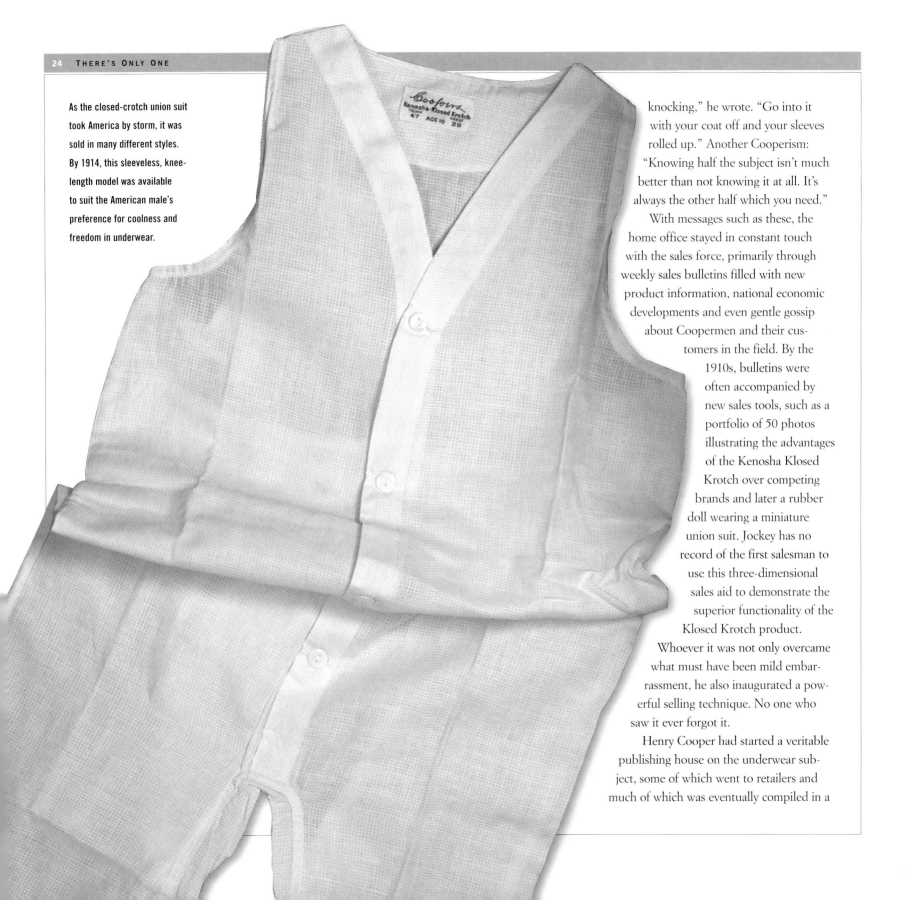

As the closed-crotch union suit took America by storm, it was sold in many different styles. By 1914, this sleeveless, knee-length model was available to suit the American male's preference for coolness and freedom in underwear.

knocking," he wrote. "Go into it with your coat off and your sleeves rolled up." Another Cooperism: "Knowing half the subject isn't much better than not knowing it at all. It's always the other half which you need."

With messages such as these, the home office stayed in constant touch with the sales force, primarily through weekly sales bulletins filled with new product information, national economic developments and even gentle gossip about Coopermen and their customers in the field. By the 1910s, bulletins were often accompanied by new sales tools, such as a portfolio of 50 photos illustrating the advantages of the Kenosha Klosed Krotch over competing brands and later a rubber doll wearing a miniature union suit. Jockey has no record of the first salesman to use this three-dimensional sales aid to demonstrate the superior functionality of the Klosed Krotch product.

Whoever it was not only overcame what must have been mild embarrassment, he also inaugurated a powerful selling technique. No one who saw it ever forgot it.

Henry Cooper had started a veritable publishing house on the underwear subject, some of which went to retailers and much of which was eventually compiled in a leatherette-bound book entitled *Tips and Pointers for Underwear Dealers and Their Salesmen*, a classic of early twentieth-century salesmanship. "A salesman is not born — he is made," this book declares. "An inexperienced man can be educated and trained into a retail salesman, and he will beat the socks off the born kind." *Tips and Pointers* was chock-full of technical descriptions of the manufacture of wool and cotton union suits and translated the hard information into selling points, including 16 features of the Kenosha Klosed Krotch, from sleeves to seams, from cuff to "collarette."

Most importantly to Henry Cooper, *Tips and Pointers* argued for the indispensable importance of well-fitted underwear. "Coopers don't believe in making the man fit the suit but making the suit fit the man," the book observes — along with undeniably humorous illustrations of men in ill-fitting underwear. It goes on to explain the niceties of measuring the customer for arm and leg length and rotundity of girth. These measurements corresponded to Cooper's 27 sizes offered in each of four different styles — long sleeve, short sleeve, long leg and three-quarter leg. No other underwear company had a line even approaching it.

"Making the suit fit the man" seems like an obvious promotion today. But at the beginning of the twentieth century, it represented the

Cooper Underwear advertisements attacked delicate subjects with humor, like this 1925 comic strip at right. *Tips and Pointers for Underwear Dealers and Their Salesmen*, below, contained more than its title implied. Written and published by Henry Cooper, the book explains each step in the making and selling of union suits, from fiber and fabric production, to machine sewing, to the measuring of the customer for the final sale. Published in 1922, *Tips and Pointers* is a model for anyone who equates product knowledge with success in sales.

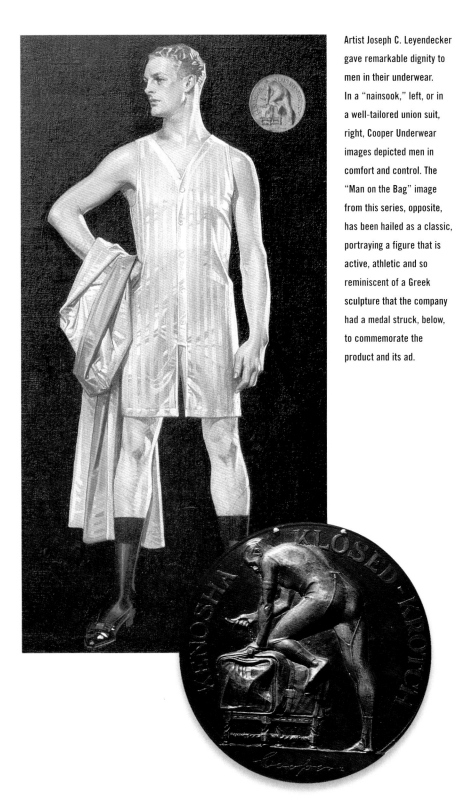

Artist Joseph C. Leyendecker gave remarkable dignity to men in their underwear. In a "nainsook," left, or in a well-tailored union suit, right, Cooper Underwear images depicted men in comfort and control. The "Man on the Bag" image from this series, opposite, has been hailed as a classic, portraying a figure that is active, athletic and so reminiscent of a Greek sculpture that the company had a medal struck, below, to commemorate the product and its ad.

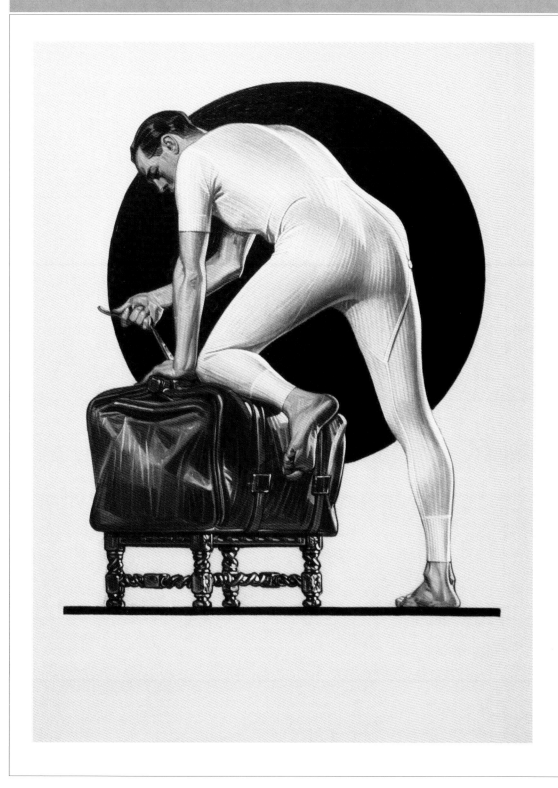

first of many steps that Cooper Underwear took in discussing a product that was considered unsuitable for public discussion at the time. Cooper's breakthrough was that whatever sensitivity American men had about their underwear was defused with mild humor, particularly in illustrations comparing poor-fitting union suits to the splendors of the Kenosha Klosed Krotch. Henry Cooper knew there was nothing funny about badly fitting underwear, unless, of course, yours fit like a charm.

The Man on the Bag

Perhaps Cooper's most significant contribution to the industry was as a pioneer in advertising. Other underwear companies had also begun advertising their wares at this time, but their messages were filled with euphemisms. Cooper was the first to make a real impact on the men's underwear market in the high-profile medium of the day — illustrated display ads in national weekly magazines.

Ads for the Kenosha Klosed Krotch broke new ground with images of men in underwear that might have been embarrassing in these times but instead were infused with pride and a commitment to quality. It was a measure of Henry Cooper's own pride and commitment, not to mention his savvy, that he chose the best illustrator available to document the stylish virtues of the Kenosha Klosed Krotch. In 1912 he hired Joseph C. Leyendecker, already famous as the creator of "The Arrow Shirt Man."

Leyendecker was also the star illustrator of *Saturday Evening Post* covers and the person after whom Norman Rockwell said he

Henry Cooper believed that treating employees like members of an extended family was the way to success. Turnover was minimal, productivity was good and Henry Cooper continued to embroider every workday with aphorisms and proverbs. Among them was his exhortation to confront opportunity with "coat off and your sleeves rolled up."

modeled his own career. Henry Cooper never claimed to be a media genius, but he knew that Leyendecker had something special. And when the artist produced Cooper's "Man on the Bag" image, it was something special too: a picture that illustrated all the product's benefits, including "form-fitting comfort" in a figure of ideal masculine distinction.

Art historians have written about this illustration of a trim male figure in a union suit with his knee on a soft-sided sports bag, applying just enough pressure to fasten it shut. Clearly, Leyendecker overcame any squeamishness about a partially dressed male; the "Man on the Bag" denotes control and athleticism so clearly that it reminded costume historian Richard Martin of the Metropolitan Museum of Art of an ancient Greek sculpture. "In this, a modern Discobolos rationalizes and valorizes a pose, denying its inherent vulnerability." In doing so, it did more than sell underwear. Cooper's "Man on the Bag" moved men's underwear resolutely into the advertising mainstream. Perhaps most importantly, the "Man on the Bag" taught Henry Cooper and a long line of successors the lesson that advertising succeeded best when it straddled the line between the sensible and the sublime.

Cooper in Charge

With its patented union suit, Cooper Underwear grew at a rate to make even the taciturn Henry Cooper smile. Sales in 1910 were $400,000. By 1915, they were on the verge of one million dollars. Through it all, Cooper never changed his basic approach. He never passed a chance to weave favorite sayings into conversations. "It is easier to do a thing right than to do it wrong" he repeated. "There is always a consumer demand for honest goods," was another nostrum. "The firm which insists that a sale is not complete until the goods are worn out and the customer still satisfied," Cooper also said, "is building a business for itself, its children and its children's children." It was hard to argue with Henry Cooper.

This old-fashioned sensibility extended to the labor situation at Cooper Underwear. "There isn't anything I enjoy more than the happiness and prosperity of the Cooper 'family,'" the president said, "and that family includes every man and woman and boy and girl that has helped us in our field of industry."

Evidence of good labor relations made newspaper headlines in 1915 when the family celebrated the opening of a new warehouse beside the 60th Street plant with "the greatest social event in the city's history," as the local paper reported. Besides food, drink and good cheer for employees and guests, the company also set up a small theater on the fourth floor of the warehouse with screen, projector and silent films of Charlie Chaplin. The tone of the Friday evening party only improved when it was announced that the next day's work at the plant was suspended, with pay, so the party could go on into the early morning hours.

Independent Enterprise

The Cooper way of treating employees was different — different enough, at any rate, from what was going on at the neighboring Black Cat plant, from which the Cooper Underwear Co. separated itself entirely in 1912. That was the year that Black Cat acquired new majority shareholders, the Allen family, who had just sold their interests in one of Kenosha's biggest leather tanning factories, and who were hatching a new plan to build a national hosiery empire.

Whatever other differences separated Henry Cooper from the Allens, the latter had an entirely different approach to labor relations. As Black Cat "modernized," for example, they practiced what was known in the textile industry as the "stretch-out" method, overworking employees on the theory that advanced machines could be operated by fewer employees. This led to labor trouble, and at Allen-A Hosiery, as Black Cat was renamed, it culminated in Kenosha's worst strike ever during the late 1920s. Henry Cooper, who had already discontinued his old White Cat label, was only too happy to be long separated from that travesty.

A Colorful Sales Force

While Cooper Underwear did its best to treat all employees like an extended family, many of its most interesting, if not eccentric, members were in sales. There was Blow Grover, for example, who sold in the Los Angeles area and became the star of the sales force, partially through seniority and partially because he was a lead player in unforgettable sales demonstrations at the company's annual sales meetings.

In one such performance, Grover played the role of a salesman trying to overcome the rudeness of a store buyer who snarls at a sample garment and throws it on the floor, where-upon Grover's dramatic skill would come to the fore. The salesman would remain silent for along time before speaking and then intoned in a low voice. "I have a great deal of respect for your store and for you," Grover would begin. "I believe your store can make a good profit selling Cooper union suits." By this point, Grover's earnestness would have everyone's attention. "So, dear sir, I ask that you treat me, my company and my products with respect...." The pitch went on, and it was often successful in the field, demonstrating that pure pride was a major ingredient in Cooper Underwear's success.

Another top man, and one close to Henry Cooper's heart, was Pete Pfarr, who came to work at Cooper Underwear in 1917 after graduating from school with a certificate in accounting. Pfarr was hired as a cashier and initially had little thought of getting into sales. But within a few years, he agreed to do what no one else was doing and call on accounts in the local area. Until then, the company sold to Kenosha and Racine stores simply by inviting retailers to the factory.

It turned out that the passive approach to nearby accounts was all wrong. So was keeping Pete Pfarr in the office as a clerk. Within six months, Pfarr had opened 35 new accounts, and he became a top-selling Cooper salesman for a long time to come. "I don't stop showing and selling until I get an order," Pfarr once said. He was a prime example of one of Henry Cooper's favorite sayings: "A salesman is not born — he is made." And Cooper was never reluctant to hold Pete Pfarr up as proof of his own time-tested ideas about success.

Industrial photography and postcard views of Coopers in the 1920s showed that Cooper Underwear conducted an orderly and prosperous business. The ladies at the end of each table are quality inspectors who tested seams and used measuring sticks to assure each garment's conformity to original patterns. Despite hard times in textiles in the 1920s, the quality of the products never changed.

Retrenchment

American men didn't just accept the new union suit from the Cooper Underwear Company, they embraced it. For nearly a decade, the Kenosha Klosed Krotch — in wool, cotton and even silk — remained America's best-selling brand of men's underwear. Company sales shot up from $400,000 in 1910 to $3 million in 1920, proving that Cooper Underwear was the key to good profit for retailers and optimal comfort for users.

Growth on this scale had everything to do with the closed-crotch design, a patent that frequently drew the company into court to fight infringers. Still, Henry Cooper knew that such dazzling success with this or any product could not last indefinitely (though royalties for the design continued to flow in for decades to come). By the 1920s, union suits were being associated with the older generation; the president clearly saw that the underwear market was changing, and Cooper was eager to develop lighter, less cumbersome underfashions fashions to change with it.

War Boosts Production

Cooper Underwear was slow to find a dominating style to replace the union suit. World War I, which America entered in 1917, delayed any major fashion shift in America, as most apparel companies were kept busy with government contracts for uniforms and

UNCLE BOB
WESTINGHOUSE
STA. K.Y.W.
THE KIDDIES
FRIEND

In the 1910s and 1920s the Cooper Underwear sales force went out with stacks of instructional photos that could be left at stores, making sure that every menswear retailer was a proper representative of the company's promise of a perfect fit. Right, the reasons for new underwear fashions were diverse. They included a new taste for government-issue skivvies that doughboys wore during the war. By the 1920s, Coopers gave these new, comfortable styles a fashionable look that was a far cry from grandpa's underclothes.

matériel that were anything but fashion-forward. At a time when Cooper design people might otherwise have searched for and developed new products, the war was forcing the company to raise production of the waning styles by several notches — and to do so quickly.

The company did not ignore the future, however. While most American manufacturing concerns simply transferred production capacity to a wartime footing, Cooper Underwear took a more ambitious approach, which was to increase capacity to serve both military and civilian demand. The company's retail base had been built through long, hard work, and management, not to mention the

sales force, was intent on preserving old customers at all costs. Thus, a substantial production increase was necessary to supply civilian demand and to respond to the national emergency and foreign war.

Henry Cooper's enthusiasm for more output did not mean that it came easily. Difficulties began with Kenosha's overburdened labor market. Local manufacturing had been growing throughout the decade, and Kenosha's industrial base was one of the fastest growing in the state (second to the shipyards in Superior). Now that several thousand Kenosha men had enlisted in the military, and everyone else was working at

full capacity, labor became a major issue at Cooper Underwear, as it was everywhere else.

Cooper responded by looking beyond Kenosha, and in 1918 the company opened a second factory across Lake Michigan in Dowagiac, Michigan, not far from old Cooper Wells in St. Joseph. Dowagiac not only had an ample supply of labor, it was also closer to sources of wool, which became more difficult to get as commodities were rationed. In theory, the satellite operation was a sound idea, but to get it up and running involved a bit of trial and error. The problem was that Dowagiac was new to the knitting and sewing industry, and the learning curve for knitters and sewers turned out to be distressingly slow. This became obvious in a few months, whereupon Henry Cooper moved the operation to Manistee, Michigan, north of St. Joseph on the lake. Here, the town provided the incentive of a free building as well as experienced textile workers. The Manistee plant was quickly producing union suits along with other underwear styles, including woven undershorts that the army ordered for warm-weather use by soldiers summering in France.

Lessons in Loyalty

The armistice of November 1918 signaled the end of the military side of Cooper Underwear's business. The next battle the company faced was to maintain sales volume at the levels that had been achieved during the war. To that end, the company increased the size of its national sales force and expanded its advertising campaign in the nation's biggest magazines, such as *Liberty*, *Colliers* and *American Legion Monthly*.

Advertising kept Coopers (the company often used the plural to emphasize its family origins) in the limelight, but staying on top of the underwear business depended on the people who had done yeoman's work for nearly two decades. Among them was the hardworking and highly trained sales force. Coopermen, as they were called, boasted superior product knowledge and could talk easily about techniques such as the difference between tubular (seamless) and full-fashioned (sewed with seams) knitting. They understood the machines used for flat-knit (plain) fabric or ribbed-knit wool or cotton, which grips like the top of a sock.

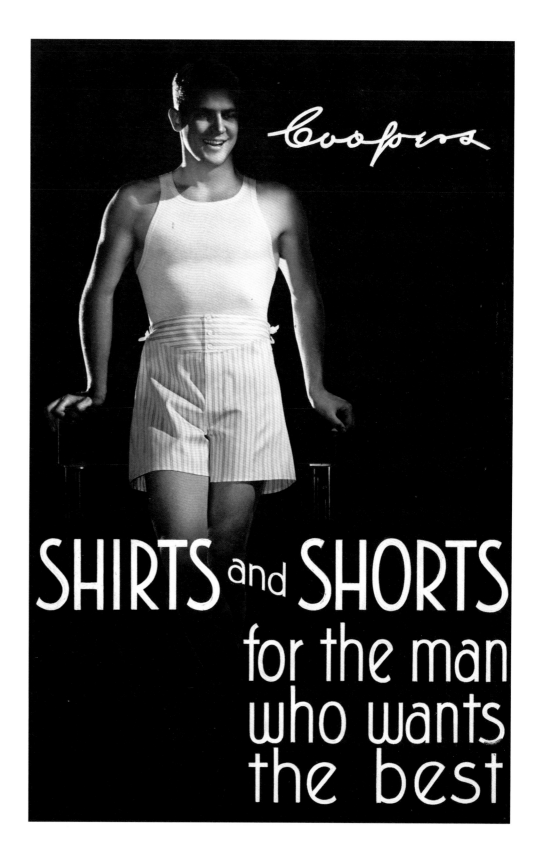

Coopers' manufacturing operation included a dye house where large rolls of cotton were fed into vats for bleaching and rinsing. The process depicted in this photo from the 1940s had changed very little since the beginning of the century.

Selling for Coopers must have seemed like a one-man traveling show, and one of its troubadours was Bob Menn, hired in 1917. Menn covered his Midwestern territories in sales trips of six or eight weeks at a time. He knew the stores and knew the products and sang the praises of both in direct proportion to the buyer's patience for his spiel. But it wasn't just the performance that sold underwear, Menn said. It was practical things like knowing the trains, the hotels and the local livery services that could haul Coopers sample trunks from point A to point B. Most of all, it was knowing and believing in a superior product, even as the product line began to change.

Shortly after the war, the Kenosha Klosed Krotch finally went into eclipse. Reasons were many, some logical, others unforeseen. One was the mass-production of cast-iron bathtubs, which began just before World War I and soon made daily bathing, while not yet *de rigueur*, at least possible in the typical middle-class home. Among the advantages of a daily bath was that a full-body suit of undergarments was no longer necessary to keep outer garments relatively fresh.

At the same time, young American men had found a replacement for the union suit. Veterans were now returning stateside with a preference for the woven boxers and a sleeveless ribbed-knit "skivvie shirt," styles that were military issue during the war. And while doughboys were not distinguished by frequent use of cast-iron bathtubs on the front or even when they got home, boxers and skivvy shirts gave the wearer a sense of freedom that the Roaring Twenties would only encourage.

Another underfashion of the moment was something called the "nainsook," a one-piece, sleeveless and short-legged garment introduced just before World War I by a company called Bradley, Voorhus and Day. Nainsooks were named after their light cotton fabric and nicknamed "BVDs" in honor of their inventor.

Cooper Underwear manufactured and sold this variety of undergarments but without the dominating edge they enjoyed with the closed-crotch design. Moreover, the underwear market became more competitive than ever, as scores of manufacturers struggled to replace wartime volume with peacetime orders. Thus, the postwar years represented a rough time for the once-towering presence of Coopers.

Added to merchandising and marketing problems was a longer-term trend that was changing the economics of manufacturing. It was the continued migration of textile mills to the South, where the Confederacy was now a faint memory, but where its painfully slow reconstruction was dependent upon cheap labor and cotton mills. The Southern textile industry was still growing in the 1920s, a decade which was prosperous for most American industries, but not for Northern textile mills. Coopers was one of the lucky survivors, but sales were on a slide. Volume of $3 million in 1920 went to less than $2 million the following year, and times would be tough for several years to come.

It was a discouraging time for Henry Cooper in particular. As early as 1913, he had tried to step down as president to give his son Robert S. Cooper an opportunity to run the family business. But in 1920 Henry was still running things and blaming himself for current troubles. He was agonizing, in particular, over a decision he had made during the war — to remain loyal to all established retail customers despite supply and demand that made it a seller's market. Loyalty to established accounts was an article of faith with the company, even when some other Coopers executives heartily disagreed.

"This was probably the greatest mistake our company made in World War I," wrote Bob Menn years later. "In making it, we missed our major opportunity for progress in distribution selection." How come? "Loyalty can become a one-way street," Menn wrote. Henry Cooper had kept the weak accounts in product during the war, but afterward, as surpluses brought prices way down, many of the same retailers gave Coopers the cold shoulder to save a few cents per dozen.

It was an ugly realization for Henry Cooper, and in dismay he wrote an open letter and sent it to a number of trade magazines. In it, he recounted the strains that his company had endured to serve all customers fairly during the war. Then he revealed how these acts of goodwill were repaid: Retailers abandoned the loyal supplier, and did so with little regard for quality. In a memorable bit of prose, Cooper ended each

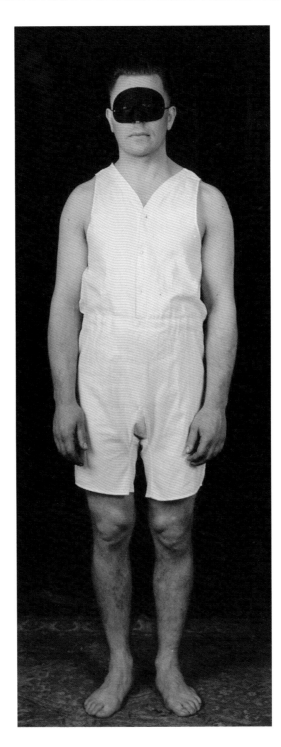

Modern photography showed retailers what Cooper's products looked like and how they should fit. Masks concealing the model's identity enabled the photographer to make the views more explicit than was otherwise proper.

paragraph of this strongly worded letter with the same line: "Were we wise, or were we damn fools?"

Perhaps Cooper was wise after all. The letter was widely read in the trade, and for decades it was cited by colleagues as a sign of straight shooting. Inside the company, it taught Cooper family members and other employees another lesson that they never forgot, that retailer loyalty is a phantom and new products, the coin of the realm in retailing, are what keep customers buying.

Battling Back

Under Robert Cooper, the company battled back by sending its vaunted sales force out with something new in 1921 — a full line of socks and stockings for men, women and children. The company did not manufacture hosiery, rather it purchased the product from contract mills. But the line had a long history at Coopers, sold well and now added considerably to company revenues. It should be mentioned that there was an additional motivation for Coopers to get back into hosiery. It was competition — some might say treachery — from the family's former partners at Allen-A Hosiery. Allen-A had recently added underwear to their product catalog and called it "Cooper," justified by the fact that the company had purchased a Vermont sewing machine company called Cooper-Bennington, which was unrelated to any Coopers from Kenosha.

This attack elicited Henry Cooper's combative streak. Trying to enjoy retirement at his farm called Dunmovin near Kenosha, he counseled his son to make as aggressive a mark as possible in hosiery, with a prominent sales office in New York and an expansive line. While these products were not difficult to buy from Southern mills at good prices, the sales force quickly put Coopers on the map as one of the two or three largest distributors of socks and stockings in the country, a position which it held for several years in the 1920s.

Were they wise, or were they damn fools? Cooper Underwear was maintaining its position as a firm with a national presence. The company was strengthening relations with better retailers, especially as they kept their products out of the growing chain stores such as Sears Roebuck and J. C. Penney. And they maintained their precious sales organization largely intact during the hardest times the company had seen since the death of Willis and Charles.

There was nevertheless a feeling in the Cooper family that the company was moving through the Roaring Twenties like a tortoise not a hare. And while the well-off family could afford to be patient, company profits had ebbed and sometimes looked like they would disappear. Henry Cooper died in 1924, leaving Robert alone at the helm to try to pick up the company's pace. But Robert's cousin Ralph, who had worked his way from factory hand to a management position in the company, sought to take a more active role in turning Coopers around.

With a sense of goodwill that always characterized this family business, Robert and Ralph discussed the problem. Ralph pointed out that the company was in debt and was looking not too different from other textile firms on the edge of extinction. And while the

Gilbert "Gib" Lance was a grandson of Zalmon Simmons of the Simmons mattress fortune. After marrying Carlotta Cooper, daughter of Charles and niece of Henry, Simmons invested his personal capital in Coopers, Inc., in 1930, joined the business as a financial man and became an indispensable calming force in the mercurial years to come.

answer to the company's problems was not obvious, Ralph, the orphan son of the late Charles Cooper, had long exhibited a passion for the company. He had dropped out of college to work there and believed it was his destiny to run the factory that he knew so well.

It was equally clear that Robert did not share such a passion and actually preferred to move to a warmer climate and worry less about day-to-day business. So the cousins came to terms in 1928. Ralph assembled a plan to borrow money, buy a majority interest in the company from Robert and other family members and blaze new trails. Robert would move to California and run the distribution side of the company for the Western states. It was an agreeable solution except that it came on the eve of the country's worst financial panic ever. The proposed reorganization stalled as Ralph sought funds to pay his debt amid the hopelessness of the Great Depression.

Once again, the dedication of family to company manifested itself at a crucial moment. In 1930, a large infusion of cash came from Ralph Cooper's brother-in-law, Gilbert S. "Gib" Lance. Lance was a member of the Simmons clan, and was an heir to the Kenosha family's mattress fortune. After long discussions with his father and mother, not to mention his wife, Carlotta Cooper Lance, Gib Lance decided to put a large portion of his personal fortune into the once and future underwear giant. Thus, Gib Lance's money along with Ralph Cooper's love of the business joined with the heartfelt commitment of everyone else who worked at Coopers to set the company on a new and successful course.

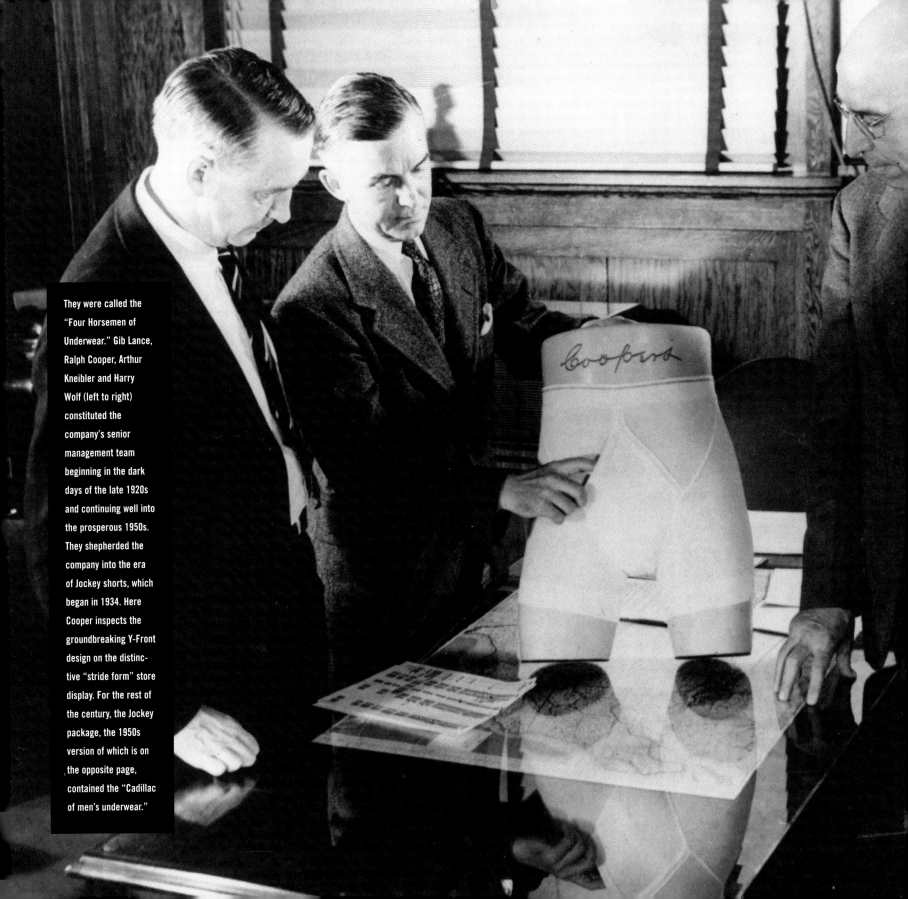

They were called the "Four Horsemen of Underwear." Gib Lance, Ralph Cooper, Arthur Kneibler and Harry Wolf (left to right) constituted the company's senior management team beginning in the dark days of the late 1920s and continuing well into the prosperous 1950s. They shepherded the company into the era of Jockey shorts, which began in 1934. Here Cooper inspects the groundbreaking Y-Front design on the distinctive "stride form" store display. For the rest of the century, the Jockey package, the 1950s version of which is on the opposite page, contained the "Cadillac of men's underwear."

The Jockey Brief

Exactly why Jockey's longtime vice president Arthur Kneibler got into the men's underwear business, he never publicly said. It may have been that anything so personal to fully half the population deserved a higher profile in the marketplace. Or perhaps he knew, when Robert S. Cooper hired him to head sales and marketing in 1928, that underfashions were once again on the verge of change.

Of course, Kneibler never had to explain himself, because not too long after he joined the company, he became known as the originator of one of the great milestones in the history of underwear, the Jockey short. This was in 1934, and in a very few years the Jockey short's dominance made the Kenosha Klosed Krotch look like a mere warm up. In fact, when Kneibler arrived, company sales were down. The underwear industry was depressed, and Coopers was surviving with commodity-priced underwear and

Arthur Kneibler was a marketing and sales expert who invented the Jockey short, the Y-Front, and promotional schemes to get underwear out in front of the consciousness of the American public. The company thought they might have the big winner they were looking for in the Singleton, a "sleek-fitting undersuit," opposite. It wasn't to be, but this advertisement was one of many that brought underwear out from the shadows and into a fashionable place in the American consumer's imagination.

ing his territory more intensely," Kneibler wrote in an article in *Sales & Marketing* magazine in 1918. "If a town is worth making at all, it is worthy of sales development."

Kneibler was also a great promoter of morale in the sales force and "a closer spirit of cooperation with the factory," he wrote. This spirit of cooperation was a two-way street, of course, and while Kneibler expected information from the field, headquarters was responsible for following up, preferably with the next innovative, indispensable and madly popular product for the salesmen to sell.

When he started at Coopers in 1928, and for several hard years during the Depression, innovation was at the top of Kneibler's to-do list. That meant finding the company's next hit, something to dominate the market as the Kenosha Klosed Krotch had done a generation before.

Introducing a new golden age at Coopers was easier said than done. The underwear trade, like most of the textile industry at this time, was filling its shelves with cheap, nameless goods from Southern mills. Coopers and everyone else at the time were competing in a market driven by price and discounts, and certainly not Cooper Underwear's traditional selling points of quality, comfort and fit. It was a frustrating process, especially for the Cadillac of men's underwear, but it was inescapable as long as Coopers' nainsooks, boxers and undershirts looked essentially like everyone else's.

Early efforts to find the next big thing fell flat, but not for lack of trying. In 1931, the company introduced a knit bag for shoes called the Shu-Pac, suitable for protecting

hosiery. When he left in 1957, there were few brands in any industry that were so known and respected the world over.

Nevertheless, joining Coopers when he did must have seemed like a strange move for a man everyone called a marketing genius. Most likely it was for the challenge of taking a once stellar company and returning it to its former glory. Perhaps he thought its hardest days were behind it. Whatever the true reason, Kneibler was a tireless worker whose first lessons in business came when he took his first job, at the age of 16, emptying wastebaskets. That position motivated him to enroll in business school in his hometown of Philadelphia.

After finishing a rudimentary commercial course, Kneibler went west and in 1910 had made it as far as St. Joseph, Michigan, (the Cooper family's old stomping grounds) where he was hired by Baker-Vawter, a major manufacturer of office filing systems. Before long, he was sales manager in charge of 200 salesmen and selling goods and services to a wide range of companies.

Part workhorse and part theoretician, Kneibler became expert at reducing the sales process to its essentials. He studied sales reports, for example, and knew which salesmen were apt to succeed simply by reviewing expenses. Spending more on hotels and less on trains was a sign the salesman was "cover-

shoes in the gentleman's closet and protecting clothes from those same shoes when packed in the gentleman's suitcase. It was a nice idea but too simple for either a patent or even a mild rush to buy them in the stores. When one Cooperman was asked about the Shu-Pac's success, he replied with a quip. "As the bachelor said of his progeny — none to speak of."

There were other promising efforts in the dark days. Coopers' best new product of 1932 was a snug ribbed-knit sweatshirt with horizontal stripes. Spiffy enough to outfit the University of Washington rowing team when they won an Olympic gold medal that year, the garment even earned the name Olympiad. It was a winner until other mills flooded the market with imitations. The next year, Coopers made a tee-shirt called the Sanitaire, a version of the short sleeved knit undershirt that was military issue during World War I. Jockey lore is that the Sanitaire was worn under the pads of the University of Southern California football team, which won the 1933 Rose Bowl. This rumor's impact on Coopers sales was negligible, however, since tee-shirts could be knocked off and churned out by the lower-cost competition.

Yet Kneibler kept imagining new styles of underwear for this period of loosened corsets and bare-chested movie stars, notably Clark Gable in *It Happened One Night*. They experimented with something they called the Snugger-Waist, a boxer short with an elastic belt (woven elastic was new) and copyrighted name. More interesting was a new-style union suit with short legs and a sleeveless top called the Singleton. Salesmen talked this one up for

Coopers

SINGLETON

The Perfect Fitting Undersuit

No Bind
No Bulk
No Buttons

its "great eye appeal... fashioned to fit every curve." But buyers pointed to the elasticized drop seat. "It's just a union suit," they said, "and they're dead as a doornail." Still, the Singleton enjoyed success, partly because union suits still had devotees and partly because of another innovation; Coopers' Singleton was mounted on cardboard and wrapped in cellophane — a first in the underwear trade — and this turned out to be a true selling point in modern self-service apparel stores.

The Singleton helped the company, renamed Coopers, Inc. in 1929, get through the Great Depression, but Kneibler was pondering the next move in mid-1934 when he received — so the story goes — a picture postcard from the French Riviera. It showed a man in a bikini-style swimsuit, and while some might have seen this as nothing but a French playboy in an unsavory pose, Kneibler saw something else: underwear for the common man. In fact, Kneibler had been talking about coming up with a modern swimsuit along these lines before he received the decisive postcard. Whatever the sequence of events, the result was the industry's biggest breakthrough ever: the design that became Jockey shorts.

Designing Success

Kneibler ran his new idea past others, including a friend and local urologist, Dr. C. W. Richards. The doctor provided particularly helpful feedback and even used a prototype on patients who had recently undergone groin surgery. Richards explained that masculine support could be beneficial for all men,

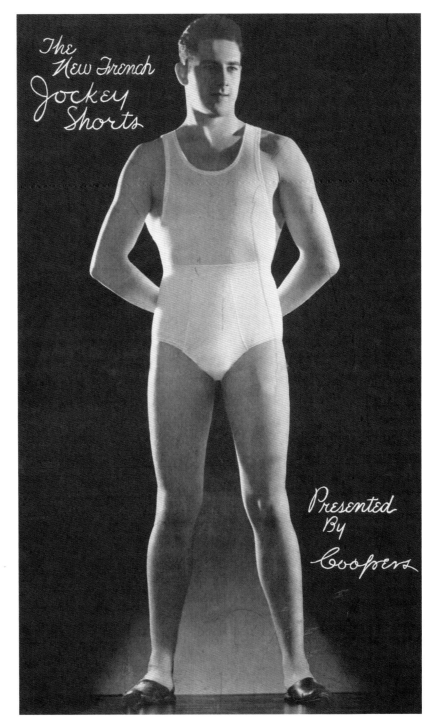

The New French *Jockey Shorts*

Presented By Coopers

At last, in 1934, Coopers introduced the product everyone was waiting for. Jockey shorts were unique, functional and snazzy enough for the post-Depression generation ready for something fashionable and new. A point-of-purchase display from 1935 shows the two vertical seams that provided Jockey's gentle but crucial element of masculine support. When the company became the first to use cellophane wrappers for underwear in 1936, the more fully evolved Y-Front was clearly visible.

though this was a delicate question, as mild support would relieve gravitational pressure on the most fragile parts of the male anatomy, but too much could constrict them.

Kneibler also went to Coopers' plant manager Herman Fredericksen, who experimented with different materials and designs for the purpose intended. Among other features, they decided on a newly developed woven elastic called Lastex for the waistband, to give the garment lift. Lastex was also used (after much trial and error) on the outside of each leg to grip the thigh and hold the garment down. By providing pressure in two directions, the garment simply and effectively did what it was meant to do while preventing the scourge of all underwear, which was crotch bind and buttock bulk.

The new undershorts looked like a winner, though Kneibler knew very well that few products sell themselves. Thus, Kneibler convened senior members of the sales force to think about how to promote what might be the company's next breakthrough product. The salesmen felt strongly that the new product should be sold at a premium price to distinguish it from the mass of cheap underwear that then dominated the market. They decided on 50 cents a pair, high by the standard of men's undergarments, but with a retail margin of more than 40 percent — they would wholesale for $3.50 per dozen — Kneibler believed the stores would have sufficient incentive to promote it enthusiastically.

A premium product needed a premium image, of course, and to set it apart, Kneibler decided to package Jockey shorts like Singletons, mounting each pair on cardboard

and wrapping it in cellophane. Kneibler knew that underwear was no longer hidden in the retailer's back room. He also remembered the success of the Singleton a year or so before, due in part to an attractive, clear package that brought unmentionables to the front of the store along with hats, shirts, belts and fancy hosiery.

The third major marketing decision for the auspicious new product was clearly the most important — the name. In the weeks before the rollout, Cooper sales managers Barrett Bates, Lou Pfarr and Bob Menn thought of little else but the perfect moniker. Among dozens of names suggested in that period, someone mentioned "Jockey," derived loosely from "jock strap," a not altogether polite word for an athletic supporter. It wasn't love at first blush, but as the sales team continued to throw out names, nothing else caused much excitement either. Then when Kneibler, mildly frustrated, asked the naming committee to write their preferences on a sheet of paper, the only name on all four lists was Jockey. It was, in retrospect, perfect — easily pronounced, athletic and suggestive of the product's masculine support.

The most important sales campaign in company history began in earnest in late 1934 with a special sales bulletin entitled "Basic Principles of Jockey Construction." Here, for the first time, Kneibler explained that Jockey was scientifically designed "such that it cannot be distorted on the body by either muscle action or the wearing of clothing over it." And on the subject of knitted fabric: "Its elasticity is needed to make Jockey conform to body lines... Its absorbent and quick

drying qualities make for both comfort and cleanliness."

Big Winner or Laughing Stock?

As the sales force had hoped, the Jockey short was an instant hit — or almost instant, as it had to overcome some doubters and also a blizzard before it exploded on the market in Chicago. In January 1935, Coopers' man on State Street got the Davis Store in Chicago, a subsidiary of Marshall Field & Co, to agree to an elaborate introduction. Displays included pictures, posters and, most conspicuously, a full-size cutout in the window of a model wearing the seemingly risqué garment. Jockey would definitely attract attention. The question was whether it would it sell or make Jockey the laughing stock of the Loop.

It looked like the latter for a moment. On the morning the windows were unveiled, Chicago was in the midst of the heaviest snowstorm in several years. It all seemed preposterous — a half-dressed model pictured in a window while Chicagoans trudged by in coats and galoshes. The store managers were quick to cancel the promotion and order the windows taken out. But before the dressers got to it, Jockey became a sensation. By noon, the store had sold out its stock of 50 dozen shorts, and in the next week, they sold 1,000 dozen.

This performance was repeated in many stores across the country. By March, a marketing magazine was reporting that "abbreviated underwear for men is indicated as a selling sensation for the warm-weather season." The *Daily News Record*, the bible of the apparel industry, referred to "an avalanche of orders from every part of the country," and Coopers was producing 3,000 dozen pairs a day by mid-spring.

Coopers had its sensation, but reaping the benefits of the new Jockey short looked as difficult as inventing it in the first place. Imitations with names like "French Snugs," "Jim-lastic" shorts and others hit the stores. An ad for "French shorts" promoted another knockoff as "the thing" for the modern gentleman. In response, Coopers quickly went on the counterattack with big ads in major magazines such as *Colliers* and the *Saturday Evening Post*. If you wanted real Jockey shorts, they stressed, you had to buy this pair.

For a while, it looked like the Jockey brand might get lost in the avalanche of imitators, and after less than a year, inventories in the Kenosha warehouse were accumulating to precarious levels. Production was drawn back, and some even suggested that price-cutting was in order. But Kneibler said no. Top-of-the-line products deserved top prices, he said. Short-term competitive distress would be overcome.

While the sales force debated the issue of price protection, people in Kenosha were confident that Jockey would rise above the competition. They knew better than anyone that the Jockey design was deceptively simple, though construction had to be precise. Seams that rose up each leg were critical to the garment's support. The elastic on the leg had to be perfect. Indeed, only a Jockey fit like a true Jockey, and that became the company line, repeated like a mantra by traveling salesmen and eventually by retail sales people in the stores.

A big part of the success of Jockey underwear was its individual packaging, which made the potentially embarrassing process of buying underwear as easy as picking up the morning newspaper. Here, two Kenosha employees place each pair of briefs in paper envelopes, a temporary alternative to cellophane used during World War II.

Many retailers, including this St. Louis department store, Farrow-Parr Company, liked the fashionable new look that the Jockey line brought to floor displays. They also didn't mind the high margins built into a product that took men's underwear out of the low-price commodity category and brought stylish profits. Cooper's 1940s sales convention, where the Jockey Boy icon was first introduced, merited front-page coverage in the *Kenosha Evening News*, opposite.

The New World

Before the Depression had run its course, Coopers had taken men's undergarments to new levels of innovation. The original Jockey short was only the beginning of a revolution that was beginning in Kenosha. It was followed by an array of related products leading in directions where other underwear manufacturers feared, or never really thought, to tread.

Parade of Products

In 1935 came the Y-Front, the crotch opening in Jockey products that became, and continues to be, the company's most recognizable feature. Y-Front construction came about after it was discovered how successful masculine support had become, but that not everyone was ready for underwear which looked like it came from the beaches of the French

In its first decade or two, masculinized Jockey was mainly an adult line — with a different model for every need — from Briefs to Midways to Longs. Youngsters grew up dreaming of the day that they could wear their dads' "Jockeys" too, and by the early 1950s, the company introduced the Jockey Junior line to take advantage of enormous pent-up demand for boys' underwear.

Riviera. Thus Kneibler sought to design something with the same features of support but in longer models and to devise a fly opening to make that possible.

The Y-Front evolved from the knowledge that the main support in the original Jockey short, which had no opening, was carried by the seams that ran up the front of each leg. The Y-Front, in effect, slightly shifted the direction of this truss work. Invented in the sample rooms in Kenosha, the opening was closed with a reinforced flap on one side of the crotch and an identical-looking hem on the other — these being the branches of the inverted Y. As explained in a sales bulletin, "The two side stems of the Y carry the weight to the upright portion of the letter which is

attached to the elastic belt of the garment." With this, the wearer could position the waistband in any comfortable position and achieve the desired level of masculine support.

The Y-Front enabled the design of a range of Jockey products with longer legs — Midways, Overknees, Longs — and a period of creativity in merchandising and marketing that the industry hadn't seen since the Klosed Krotch days. "Customer-driven" was not yet in the vocabulary of salesmen, but Cooper Underwear took an indisputable lead in making what they sold instead of vice versa. New products and new ways of selling them came at a furious pace. While relations between the manufacturing and marketing were not always silky-smooth (Secretary-Treasurer Gib Lance

often said that his most important job was to keep President Ralph Cooper, who ran the factory, from assaulting Kneibler, and vice versa) fast-rising sales were a fine palliative. Coopers became, without question, the creative center of the underwear universe.

Credit also went to salesmen in the field who were smart and persistent, as evidenced by a 1936 promotion at Wieboldt's, an important Chicago area department store chain at the time. In this case, the retailer agreed to an in-store campaign to introduce the complete Jockey line, and then balked at the last moment. This had Art Kneibler on the next train to Chicago to find out why Wieboldt's cancelled the event.

After high-level discussions, Kneibler

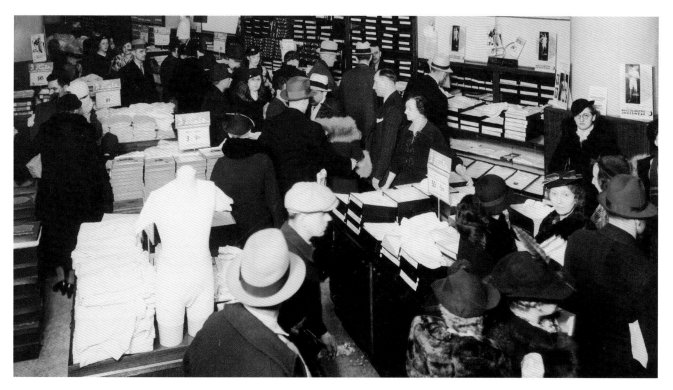

The 1936 Wieboldt's store promotion proved to this important Chicago retailer that selling Jockey underwear was very good business indeed. Throughout this period, very few products of any kind generated the kind of recognition that the Jockey line did.

Always eager to challenge convention, but not good taste, Cooper's Cellophane Wedding at a 1938 apparel market in Chicago demonstrated that the well-dressed man — with his bride at his side — had Jockey underwear on underneath.

came back with good news — that he had revived the sales event and that it was bigger than before. Wieboldt's management was convinced when Kneibler made a point-by-point case for Jockey and promised support of the sales event that included training for the retail sales staff. The store had been afraid of something so new; Kneibler convinced them that Jockey's unique countertop displays would sell underwear like Wieboldt's had never sold underwear before. And to make sure of it, Kneibler sent his most loquacious salesmen to be present for the promotion to talk about underwear with a passion unknown in men's accessories at the time.

"Not only did it add substantially to our volume," wrote the Wieboldt's merchandise manager when the event was over, "but it has given us a new idea in men's underwear merchandising." No one could credit any but the Jockey brand for bringing underwear out in the open, which it did by meeting an obvious need (male support) not to mention offering a 40 percent markup for the retail stores. At Wieboldt's, at any rate, underwear thus made its odyssey from back room to the countertop and wasn't turning back.

Catching the Public's Eye

Within a year or two, Coopers had secured Jockey's position as the nation's most popular line of nether garments, and Arthur Kneibler became something of an unlikely celebrity in the apparel industry. "From this glum countenance come scintillating thoughts," wrote the *Milwaukee Journal* in 1938 under a photo of Kneibler doing his best to smile. He was known as "the man who chased droopiness

out of drawers," in the *Journal's* words. But Kneibler, who had a short temper as well as sullen moments, also knew that changing America's underwear was a tireless task.

Shortly after the Wieboldt promotion, the next big idea from Jockey was a plaster-cast half-mannequin called, perhaps euphemistically, the "stride form." Stride meant that the torso assumed a position with the right leg extended slightly, but this was hardly the most remarkable or noticeable thing about it. What was entirely new in the world of in-store displays was the inclusion of male contours, vital in order to show off the benefits of the Jockey line but potentially shocking to more sensitive viewers. In fact, a few complained. "Obscene and offensive," said the most vociferous, but such flap only attracted attention to what was an otherwise chaste manner of promoting a garment. And it sold. Stores ordered the stride form by the thousands.

Then there was perhaps Jockey's biggest attention-getter of all, the so-called "Cellophane Wedding." This might have been the most dazzling single event in the history of underwear marketing. It was a style show that opened the 1938 convention of the National Association of Retail Clothiers and Furnishers. A bride and groom appeared in transparent evening clothes, the better to see their undergarments. Again, this might have seemed a risky thing. But to Art Kneibler it was another well-aimed effort to create a new image for men's underwear, in this case, Jockey Briefs and a contoured undershirt that the smiling groom wore beneath his see-through tux. When the Cellophane Wedding hit the newspapers in the days that followed,

The Cellophane Wedding and subsequent ads, like the one above, featured in *Esquire* in 1939, received international publicity and also reminded consumers that Jockey underwear was not hidden in the back of the store but was first to come out front in cellophane packaging. The only negative note that anyone remembered was from Germany, where the Nazi propaganda machine used it as a supposed example of American decadence.

The Jockey table display was invented by salesman Pete Pfarr as a way of organizing the increasing array of Jockey products for a Racine department store. "Man, did that contraption ever sell Jockeys," Pfarr said, and the sales department quickly had this handsome model worked up.

it generated all the good-natured humor that Jockey's glum genius intended. Its only public detractor was reported to be a Nazi newspaper in Germany that ran a photo as further proof that the decadent, depraved Western democracies were out of control — but did little to put American customers off.

Despite this critique, Jockey continued to sell marvelously. In 1937 Coopers' sales hit the $3 million level and went to $4 million in 1939 and $5 million in 1940, when net profits exceeded $300,000. What had been a small, struggling Kenosha firm in the beginning of the Depression had not only weathered the storm but made the industry's greatest strides despite the economy. It was a credit to optimism, which was always a Cooper family specialty, although Arthur Kneibler was never satisfied with anything quite so subjective.

Kneibler insisted, now as always, on hard information, market data about where, to whom and how much Jockey underwear was selling. With a thoroughness that exasperated his colleagues, the vice president mapped Jockey's success by connecting the numbers, not only from sales figures and the results of past promotions, but in specially developed marketing surveys. He hired

youngsters, some of them future Coopermen, to travel the country and ask the questions that he constantly asked himself.

The findings were enlightening. In the late 1930s, for example, they revealed that despite the enormous early success of Jockey shorts, only 8 percent of consumers in America had heard of the product. This was news, if not to Kneibler, then to the salesmen who complained when sales took normal and periodic downturns. Numbers showed that harder work would pay off, as most male consumers interviewed also said they might give masculine-support underwear a try. "There's a large untapped market out there," Sales Manager Bob Menn told his salesmen.

Listening to Shoppers

Information led to new ideas and more promotions. One towering sales innovation of the time was the result of a brainstorm of Pete Pfarr, whose customers were happy with Jockey sales but struggling to display the variety of Jockey products. The solution to this problem came with crystal clarity as Pfarr was filing papers in his office one day — it was a countertop underwear display with labeled tabs dividing the packages according to style and size. Pfarr built the first dispenser himself and placed it in one of his better stores in Racine, Wisconsin. "Man did that contraption ever sell Jockeys like Jockeys were never sold before," Pfarr later remembered. "After a day or two, I told Mr. Kneibler of my experience. He took the idea, and before long we got a fine Jockey dispenser to distribute to the trade."

Good retailing was only part of the battle, of course. Advertising was equally important,

Department store displays in the 1930s were sleek and streamlined, as evidenced by this photo of Baum's Department Store in Green Bay, Wisconsin. But surveys in the late 1930s revealed that despite booming sales of Jockey shorts, only 8 percent of American consumers had heard of them. Cooper Underwear and its all-important sales force, known as Coopermen, worked hard to sell "through" their retail customers to the receptive public.

and here too Coopers broke new ground, challenging the public's squeamishness about underwear by using the same combination that had worked in the past: a straightforward message and first-class illustration. Was underwear embarrassing? Not when it fit, said Ralph Cooper, who pointed to his Uncle Henry's "Man on the Bag" as proof.

In this spirit, Coopers added an additional feature, mild humor, to create Jockey's most successful campaign of the 1930s, the "squirmer" campaign. The ads featured photos and drawings of men suffering from bulk and bind, these ads showed what happened to men not wearing Jockey shorts. The ads were a long-running success for many reasons; among them was skilled and well-known illustrator Peter Arno, who also drew covers for the *New Yorker*. One of Arno's memorable drawings showed a dinner party with an otherwise well-dressed gentleman squirming in his undergarments and his wife casting a disapproving glance. "Are you a squirmer?" the ads asked.

The squirmer campaign constituted a major step forward also because it targeted women as well as men. The ads were using what Coopers had learned in the surveys, that women were frequent buyers of men's underwear. The squirmer campaign suggested that even if men did not care if they occasionally tugged on their underwear in public, their wives certainly did. The ads also suggested that a man's comfort might be his own responsibility, but his behavior...? Well, that was his wife's concern. If Jockey underwear could influence his comportment for the better, then, no purchase in a man's wardrobe could be more obvious or useful.

Ah, the squirmer campaign! In a world where underwear was considered "unmentionable," Jockey introduced some not-so-gentle irony in the relative comforts and discomforts of men's underwear. As the illustrations show, the real triumph of this campaign was in its direct appeal to women, who were the primary shoppers for men's underwear — and quite interested in keeping their men in comfortable underwear.

The world of Coopermen was an orderly, well-dressed and happy one in the post-World War II era, when the sales force was growing and no one was more welcomed by the nation's menswear buyers. The sales convention of 1950, at which this photo was taken, was held at the Elks Club in Kenosha. The point of purchase image shown opposite reflected the notion that in an era of prosperity, the store had a full inventory of America's best underwear.

Wider Horizons

The strength of Jockey underwear was in the exquisite simplicity of the idea — the way the fabric, the design and even the name all worked together toward the overarching objective of comfort. A product of such distinct form and function was rare in any era, and the one member of the management team who understood just how rare was Harry H. Wolf Sr. Wolf, owner of the national accounting firm, Wolf and Company, began his relationship with Coopers as corporate auditor, but his fascination with the Jockey concept motivated him, over a period of decades, to buy the company.

Enter Harry Wolf

Harry Wolf could hardly have predicted that underwear would be his métier, but as an accountant and management consultant with a growing practice, he enjoyed a unique view

Harry Wolf began his relationship with Coopers as the company's outside auditor. He is pictured at right with the accountants who worked for him. By the 1950s he was the controlling stockholder of Coopers, which would remain a family business.

of many different kinds of industries. In each one, ranging from newspapers and textiles to tire makers and machine tools, he began as an auditor but studied the dynamics of his clients' businesses so deeply that he became a kind of philosopher-sage.

Wolf began work with Coopers, Inc. in 1930 when the company was awash in red ink. Secretary-Treasurer Gib Lance was in Chicago at the Continental Bank, where loan officers were cordial to Lance, quite naturally, but less than sanguine about Coopers' present financial condition. The bankers suggested

that what Coopers needed was a good consultant. They suggested Wolf and Company, with offices a few doors down from the bank.

Harry Wolf took on the assignment and, after intensive study, declared that the state of the company was imperfect, but its position was strong, and positive change was possible. Lance could only agree, and by the following year, 1931, Lance asked Wolf to execute a list of changes that he had recommended. Wolf agreed to do so and also agreed, with astonishing confidence, that

his compensation should be based on the company's performance.

From the beginning, Wolf's intervention was simple but forceful. Jockey lore has it, for example, that the first thing Wolf did as consultant was fire every employee in the company on Friday and announce that all positions were open to all applicants on Monday. In fact, most employees got their old jobs back, though at a considerable cut in pay. Because the Depression was on and jobs were hard to find, Harry Wolf's gambit caused no revolt and instantly improved the bottom line.

Simple Strengths and a Broad Market

Harry Wolf then became even more intrigued with the company after the introduction of Jockey shorts. By the mid-1930s, he was a member of the board, though not yet a stockholder of the company, which was still owned by Coopers and Lances. Wolf saw, and frequently articulated, the company's unique strengths, including "brand support... a name that means something to those who use it," as he described in a speech at the 1938 Coopers sales convention. This was the result, he concluded, of unique products and skillful advertising — a combination of assets as valuable as it was rare.

Wolf also praised Jockey's "simplified line and broad market," that had evolved because of "intelligent development of new numbers and just as aggressive action toward the elimination of proven slow and unprofitable numbers," he said. Coopers had long distinguished itself in this and other aspects, which included "style leadership," he said, and "financial and moral support of constant style research." Wolf stressed that such strengths were fundamental to the company's future. "Most companies that you regard as successful haven't more than sixty percent of the success factors that you have," Wolf declared.

It was more than just talk. With Wolf as a consultant, Jockey added several successful numbers to the Jockey product line, which already included Briefs (a more specific term than "shorts"), Midways, Overknees and Longs. It introduced the highly useful "Bellin," a brief with an abdominal-support waistband. Jockey also reintroduced the tee-shirt, whose loose-fitting good looks would

explode as a fashion statement a few years later when Gene Kelly wore one in *Anchors Aweigh* (1945) as did Marlon Brando in *A Streetcar Named Desire* (1947).

A combination of the old and new was fundamental to a successful enterprise, Wolf said, and it turned out to be advice for the ages. "Success is organic — something that grows out of the past," he said. "It grows from within. The small successes budding from sturdy central successes of right management and sound organization."

Wolf believed it sincerely, and so armed in the mid-1930s he made one of his first visits to a bank on Coopers' behalf. Wolf was asking for $275,000, the amount still needed to manufacture and market the company's new line. In conference with the bankers, Wolf described Coopers' retail network, which was solid due in large part to the good profit margins built into Jockey pricing. He also talked about the company's innovative new products and the excitement that was already being generated by the sales force. The bankers nodded, impressed, and then asked the question that Wolf was waiting for: "What collateral do you have?"

"My good name," replied Harry Wolf, and the loan was granted.

Clearly, Harry Wolf went way beyond the call of duty as auditor-consultant. He was

Here in 1939 Dick Jensen models the Bellin, a style that provided superior abdominal support. Jensen rose to become president of Jockey International in the 1970s.

In 1940, the Jockey Boy image symbolized pride in the brand. The original bronze figure was just short of one foot in height, and it was reproduced to precise dimensions in the point-of-purchase figure here. The Jockey Boy was a durable symbol. It evolved into a realistic figure in silks, opposite, in the early 1960s, then to the more minimalist "half-boy" figure of recent years.

Jockey
THE FAMOUS BRAND OF SUPPORT UNDERWEAR
T.M. REG. U.S. PAT. OFF.

Y-FRONT–PATENT OF COOPERS Inc.

MODERN
2-PIECE
KNITTED

STYLES
FOR ALL
OCCASIONS

NO GAP
OPENING

WEARING KEEPS
IT CLOSED

SUPPORT FROM THE BELT

devising policies that would carry the company forward for years to come. Wolf made sure, for example, that Coopers invoked fair trade laws that could govern retail prices on all Jockey products. Slightly higher prices, he insisted, kept the line distinct in the eyes of retailers and the public alike, and by enforcing fair-trade contracts, which were affirmed by the Miller-Tydings Amendment to the federal Sherman Anti-Trust Act in 1937, Coopers kept discounters from undermining a profitable and high-end image.

Protecting and Promoting the Idea

Wolf engineered Jockey's marketing plan in other ways. He placed patent and copyright issues in the hands of high-powered attorneys, rightly believing that the Jockey name was fundamental to its success. Thus, Chicago lawyer James Hume reviewed anything that was written about the product from an early date in the interests of preserving the valuable, though potentially fragile, trademark.

Specifically, Hume curtailed any claim that Jockey shorts were for athletes as "a glorified jock strap," the lawyer later explained. "Descriptiveness is the fatal disease" of many trademarks; most courts would disallow trade names like "racer" or "jockey" if they described too specifically what they did or who they were for. In this vein, Hume's gatekeeping over early advertising began the long process of building the Jockey name not just in the market but in the court of trademark law as well.

Hume went on to counsel that threats to the trademark could be minimized if the well-known Jockey name were tied inextrica-

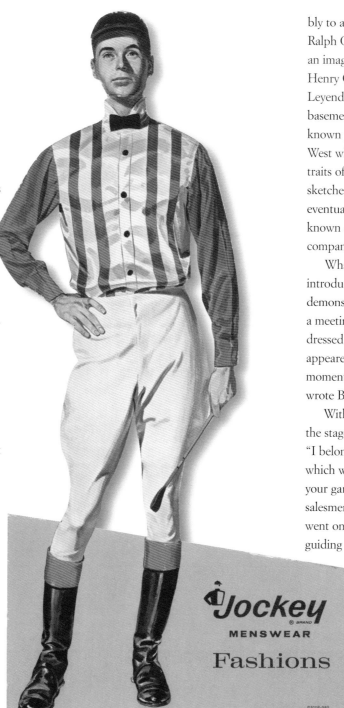

bly to an equally well-known image. Thus Ralph Cooper sought an artist to create such an image, and guided by the experience of Henry Cooper, who had hired Joseph Leyendecker, Ralph did not go to the bargain basement. He chose Frank Hoffman, a well-known painter and sculptor of the American West who showed particular skill in his portraits of horses and riders. After several sketches, Hoffman produced a figure, and eventually a bronze statue, that became known as the *Jockey Boy*. It served as the company's trademark for five decades.

Whatever else this image represented, its introduction at the 1940 sales convention demonstrated sheer confidence. It was during a meeting of the sales force when a live actor dressed similarly to Hoffman's figure appeared in "one of the most dramatic moments in Jockey sales convention history," wrote Bob Menn.

With great fanfare, the actor walked on the stage. "I am Jockey," he said, then paused. "I belong in the future... I am a trademark which will forever distinguish your name and your garment in the minds of buyers." The salesmen were impressed, and the Jockey Boy went on. "I am your inspiration and your guiding star," the Jockey Boy said finally. "I'll be seeing you in store windows all over the country."

While the trademark did not face any early challenges in the U.S., patent battles, a separate but related issue, were a pressing concern almost from the beginning. In fact, early imitators of Jockey Briefs never really came close to Coopers' patented design — it appeared they did not understand what made the Jockey products so comfortable. Yet Coopers did appear as defendant in an infringement case in the late 1930s, and it turned out to be James Hume's initiation as legal defender of the "masculin-ized" realm.

Finally settled in 1940, the case concerned a Cleveland apparel designer named Paolucci who claimed that he owned the patent for any garment that provided masculine support, and that Jockey violated it. Paolucci's design was a boxer short with an inside liner which some called a "hammock," functioning much like the inside shell of a men's bathing suit of today. The case threatened a whole range of Jockey products and was especially serious when Coopers lost at the district court level in Ohio. Hume's first case for Coopers was the appeal, and as he studied the problem, he noted something crucial — that it was impossible to illustrate the true function of a Jockey if no one was wearing it. This looked like an insuperable problem, however, since close inspection of the garment was impossible if someone *was* wearing it.

Hume's observation led to what must have been one of the stranger legal briefs in appel-late court history when he arrived before the judge in Cincinnati with three-dimensional models of a pair of Jockey shorts and a pair of Paolucci's. Made of copper sheeting, Hume's metal underwear was designed to demonstrate the construction and function of both gar-ments. Once he got them to court — not itself a simple matter as the exhibits required a sep-arate sleeping berth on the overnight train from Chicago — he maintained his demeanor,

delicately highlighted the construction and pressure points of the Jockey shorts, and prevailed.

Selling Through

The early success of Jockey underwear created delivery and supply problems for a company that was suddenly faced with unprecedented volume. But the company naturally regarded this problem as an opportunity, seizing it initially by educating store managers and buyers to order Jockey products in a timely and regular way. More and more salesmen were finding that when Jockey underwear sold out, the shelves were left empty. This inspired Al Valenzuela, a Cooperman based in California, to make a scientific study, beginning by counting stock, his own and competitive brands, at each of his accounts. Over a period of several months, he calcu-lated the results and discovered something that he was happy to make known to anyone who would listen. It was that in nearly 100 stores in Southern California, 70 percent of the underwear sales were of Jockey products, an impressive figure except for the fact that these same stores had 76 percent of their inventory in other brands.

Salesman Lou Pfarr, Pete's brother, found a similar situation in Milwaukee in stores where he was often badgered by retail sales people. "Whenever I came into the store," Pfarr said, "the clerks usually cornered me and wanted to know why we hadn't shipped the merchandise ordered." The answer was that it hadn't been ordered. Store manage-ment was holding back, he discovered, until the slower selling underwear sold out too.

"Something new and different had to be done," said Pfarr, who later became national sales manager. What they needed, and what Coopers certainly wanted, was to separate the reordering of Jockey from the slower selling brands.

So began Coopers' "model stock control program" which consisted of counting inven-tory in all stores on a regular basis, document-ing sales, and making sure that reorders were made in time to keep product available. The counting was done by the Coopermen and could be tedious work, but results proved that Jockey underwear sold better, tied up less cap-ital and was two or three times more profitable than the average product in most menswear departments. The company's model stock control created a new kind of relationship between manufacturer and retailer, and led to what Coopers referred to as the "sell through" concept. Salesmen didn't just sell product *to* the stores; they sold to the retail market *through* the stores. With this in mind, Coopers and its retail distributors remained partners in a transaction that was focused on a satisfied Jockey wearer eager to come back for more.

Jocks for Jockey

As stores got more comfortable with Jockey products, so too was the public. Not too many years before, underwear was a subject that most men preferred not to discuss. By the late 1930s, breezy banter about Jockey underwear did not replace topics like the New York skyline or trans-Atlantic air travel around the water coolers of America, but new-style undershorts did capture the public imagination in a number of ways.

Coopers was an early entrant into the world of athlete endorsements, although in the early years these tended to represent a genuine preference on the part of the endorser. In 1948, members of the British Olympic Team, hosting the Olympic Games in London that year, were supplied with Jockey underwear as part of their official wardrobe. English stores were quick to take advantage of this, as Jockey's Y-Front became inextricably connected with the five Olympic rings, representing the pinnacle of athletic form.

Sports turned out to be a surefire way of getting the attention of the men who wore, or might wear, Jockey shorts. Athlete endorsements began almost by accident at first, in 1935, when someone at headquarters learned that golf star Tommy Armour (winner of the 1927 U.S. Open) wore Jockey underwear. Mostly out of curiosity, the company contacted him, and Armour turned out to be so enthusiastic that the golfer agreed to endorse the product for a small fee. "No more hookin', slicin' underwear for me," Armour

said in ads and display cards in the stores. "The snug fit with no binding or bunching gives complete body freedom, and they are not hard to look at in the locker room."

The Tommy Armour endorsement drew enough attention that Coopers soon went out to find more sports stars. One of the most memorable ads was published in the national magazines in 1938 with Sammy Baugh, quarterback for the Washington Redskins, pictured in Jockey Longs. Football was the perfect vehicle for Longs, since the product

was seasonal, and so was football.

"Protect your hothouse legs," was the slogan beneath "Slingin' Sammy's" picture. No one could claim that Baugh's legs, which were covered, were giving Betty Grable's a run for their money. But the ad peeled away another layer of discomfort when men talked or even thought about their underwear. The happy result was that Jockey cold-weather long johns captured a dominant share of a market that other manufacturers rarely advertised and left to chance.

Jockey's international presence came unsolicited at first, as the world was drawn to Yankee styles, right down to the Jockey shorts. Before the 1930s were over, the company was plying the sea lanes of the world to sell and license Jockey products in the Americas, Europe, Australia and Asia.

Jockey the World Over

J ockey International's presence around the world has a long history. It began when the idea for the original Jockey short was borrowed from France and continued when it made America's newest underwear sensation available in Europe. By the mid-1930s, export sales constituted a small but reliable source of business, and before long, Coopers was signing contracts with overseas partners who built strong local markets for Jockey products on their own. This was the beginning of the company's licensing program, which demonstrated that quality products, along with sound marketing practices, knew no borders.

The First License

Even before World War II, U.S. products were regarded as something special the world over. So along with movies, autos, skyscrapers and other American icons, Yankee underwear had distinct, if understated, appeal. Initially, it crossed the borders in advertising, particularly Jockey's ads in *Life* magazine, which was launched with wild and unexpected success in 1936. *Life* attracted readers throughout the English-speaking world, and it wasn't long before Jockey's mail included inquiries from abroad.

The first to show enthusiasm were the Canadians, whose early imports of Jockey underwear enjoyed such demand that a Canadian manufacturer, J. R. Moodie Co. Ltd., soon asked for rights to manufacture and sell the products themselves. A licensing agreement was negotiated and signed in 1936, the same year European export agents began placing orders.

Within another year, English sales had grown to the point that Ralph Cooper decided to sail across the pond himself to have a look. While in London, the president stopped at several menswear stores that stocked Jockey products. The highlight of these calls was to Simpson's, a well-regarded West End clothier, where the manager was so pleased to meet the president of Coopers that Cooper couldn't get out of the store until he had an order for 24,000 garments.

This kind of activity certainly interested Art Kneibler, who followed up a few months later with a visit of his own, this time to find candidates for a licensing agreement. With characteristic dispatch, he discovered a Scottish knitting mill that produced high-quality knit goods, largely woolens, sold in the best stores in the British Isles. The manufacturer, Lyle and Scott, received Kneibler very warmly indeed and responded that, by all means, they were interested in a license to manufacture and sell Jockey. An agreement was struck in early 1938. It was not the most propitious moment as hostilities in Europe were brewing badly, but Lyle and Scott erected a new factory just the same, near its old one in Hawick, Scotland, to manufacture cotton briefs and undershirts.

The Lyle and Scott licensing agreement faced an unexpected obstacle when the

British copyright office declined to grant exclusive use of the name Jockey. The trade name was judged to be "functionally descriptive," a fatal flaw for in trademark law in both the U.S. and the U.K. The interpretation of the British office was a stretch, certainly, as there was never a suggestion anywhere that people who rode horses preferred Jockey shorts. Nevertheless, Lyle and Scott copyrighted the more prosaic (but perhaps more English) "Y-Front," a name that has survived in Britain for decades. What did not change was the Jockey selling program — fixtures, stride forms, size charts, tape measures and sales booklets such as the Coopers' hand-out entitled "Retail Selling Made Easy," reworked for Lyle and Scott in Oxbridge English.

As the Y-Front took its place on the British underwear landscape, other license arrangements appeared on the horizon. In what is now known as the Pacific Rim, Coopers already had a functioning sales network that included Al Shelton, based in Hawaii and selling in India, the Philippines, Java and China. While it was hard to supervise Shelton from such a distance, his reputation in Kenosha got a shot in the arm thanks to Andrew Lance, Gib Lance's father. During a vacation in the Orient, Andrew Lance disembarked his ship in Shanghai and bought an English-language paper on the dock. No sooner had he opened it, than his eye landed on an ad for Jockey shorts placed by a local retailer.

Shelton knew the Pacific territory like others knew State Street in Chicago. Thus, when management asked him to seek possible licensees in Australia, he quickly identified

MacRae Knitting Mills, in Sydney, as a likely candidate. MacRae had recently developed a brand of swimwear that itself was destined for greatness, Speedo. The company's chairman, Alisdair MacRae, knew the look of a winning brand and was immediately ready to sign an agreement with Jockey. The deal was struck in 1938. MacRae Mills had quick and notable success in Australia, so much so that it inspired a pack of patent infringers. These "wolves of competition," as MacRae took to calling them, were fended off successfully, and the skirmishes, while time-consuming, did nothing to hurt the Jockey short's reputation as the most fashionable undergarment "down under."

Jockey at War

Coopers' licensing program was only one element of its success that was interrupted with the advent of World War II. Prior to the bombing of Pearl Harbor in 1941, the company had experienced double-digit growth yearly for a decade. Once the war started, the nation's industrial might was redirected largely to military production. Coopers joined in, too; the factory was immediately occupied with the first of its more than 30 military contracts during the national emergency. Some of these were related to the mill's peacetime work — some Jockey shorts, which continued to make Kenosha famous in underwear circles, but more of them were wool drawers and one-piece nainsooks that were then government issue. Another contract was for parachutes, critical military work that required the skilled hands that otherwise sewed Jockey shorts.

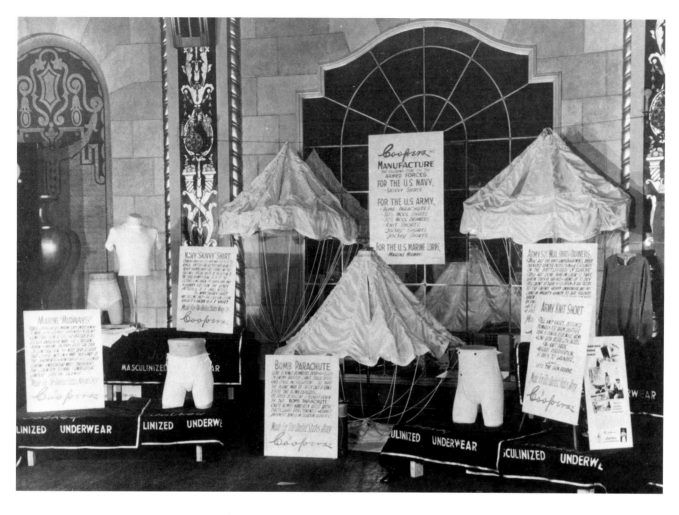

During World War II, Jockey contributed to the military effort, making ordnance parachutes and keeping men on the war front, as well as the home front, comfortable in a full range of Jockey styles. Here, the range of products turned out by the nation's most famous underwear producer are displayed at the Kenosha War Show conducted at the Eagles Club ballroom in 1945.

It was a hard time for Coopers, but the company responded with patriotic fervor. Salesmen went into the military in droves, and those who didn't enlist moved into military production jobs, with the company promising to make up any pay cut that they might suffer as a result. This policy left the organization in tatters, but it represented the kind of sacrifice that instilled loyalty. "It's an organization that will bend over backwards for everyone in the company," said Cooperman Jim Hatchett a

few years after the war. Hatchett had to give up selling Jockey shorts for a while during the war, but he never stopped selling the company to his younger colleagues.

So Jockey shorts were in short supply during the war, a situation that the company tried to turn into a positive with a series of ads in *Life*, *Saturday Evening Post* and *Esquire*. "Jockey may be hard to get" was one campaign that explained how the company had suspended a large part of its consumer pro-

duction because of its military contract. The ads were intended to build pent-up demand that could, and did, break loose when the war was over. Another wartime ad pointed out that Jockey was hard at work in the effort to win the war. "Marines come first — that's why Jockey Midways are scarce," it read, alluding to the fact that a good part of the war in the Pacific theater was being fought by Leathernecks in masculinized Midways.

While Coopers worked to maintain

In the 1946 photo at right, a Kenosha worker cuts and bundles waistbands to length. After, Coopers substituted neoprene for war-rationed natural rubber, the waistband of Jockey shorts became a source of complaint. But the company quickly replaced each defective garment to make sure customers didn't lose faith in the Jockey brand.

customer loyalty, the U.S. government came up with a plan that seemed aimed to do everything but destroy it. A proposal from the Office of Price Administration asked for the standardization of a whole range of civilian products, including underwear, according to government-set specifications and prices. Instead of Jockey, Carter's, BVD and Hanes, the public would be choosing between Grade A and Grade B and would have little reason to note or care that Jockey had once been considered the Cadillac of men's underwear.

To combat the government's proposal, Coopers sent several members of senior management to testify against it in Congress. Arthur Kneibler, for one, espoused his position that the strength of any peacetime economy depended upon brand names that drove competition. Jockey was not the only company to protest; other apparel and food companies were hard on the case, which became clear enough to the legislators that they reversed the OPA initiative before it was enacted. With this victory behind them, Harry Wolf and Robert Cooper, Ralph's young son, followed up after the war by helping to organize the Brand Names Foundation, a lobbying and public relations group that included manufacturers and the media that sold advertising to them.

While preserving brand names was a philosophical argument, preserving the Jockey reputation required endless hard work. The company's sincerity was tested shortly after the war over the question of an integral but not-particularly-noticeable element of Jockey design: the waistband. Waistbands became an issue toward the beginning of the war when

By 1947 Jockey ads were touting its improved waistband — each and every one embroidered with the Jockey name.

natural rubber, the main constituent of the original Lastex, became unavailable for consumer goods. Coopers then replaced natural rubber with neoprene, a synthetic rubber developed for a variety of heavy and light uses during the war. Before the war's end, this too became restricted, which forced Jockey to fashion the unlikely expedient of buttons in the waist of new Jockey shorts. This throwback to pre-elastic days continued for a year or two, after which Jockey loyalists were supplied with small sections of elastic that could be hooked into their austerity briefs.

All was well on the waistband front, but not for long. Trouble ensued about two years after V-J Day when the makers of neoprene changed its formula slightly in a way that was good for tire makers, synthetic rubber's largest user, but a disaster for Jockey. After a series of complaints from customers, Coopers discovered that the new neoprene broke down quickly in automatic dryers, a popular appliance in the postwar consumer age. Coopers quickly addressed this problem by going back to natural rubber. The real challenge, however, was restoring confidence in the Jockey brand among buyers whose knickers, so to speak, were in a twist. To its credit, the company replaced all defective garments without question, a program that cost the company $200,000 but saved a generation of customers. The problem was so well handled that the company took to boasting about the waistbands of its products, and by 1947 was embroidering the name "Jockey" into their waistbands ever after.

Through steady work and sacrifice, Coopers entered the postwar economic boom

In 1946, Jockey was a champion on its way to becoming a legend. No claim was too great, including an endorsement from baseball's home run king, Babe Ruth. Athlete endorsements would remain an important merchandising tool for the company in the years to come.

with its unique strengths intact. Salesmen returned from service knowing that their old jobs were waiting. Other veterans joined up in great numbers, and the company rebuilt a sales force that was unparalleled in its industry. It was poised to take advantage of the biggest economic boom in the history of the world, one in which the trusted brand names of the past were the biggest beneficiaries of all.

Continental Crusade

America's ability to recover quickly after the war was in contrast to Europe, and as European industry dug out from the rubble, many of its leaders set their sights on the United States as the successful model. In fact, Jockey shorts were being made on the Continent even before the end of the war. In 1942, Coopers contracted with Swiss licensee, Vollmoeller Knitting Works, located in Uster, just north of Zurich. Even before the war, Swiss men had a taste for Jockey shorts, and when wartime trade blockades ended the importation of luxury items like American underwear, the demand went unfilled. That was when Hans Vollmoeller negotiated the licensing agreement with management in Kenosha; the details were settled by mail and Teletype.

With ingenuity to spare, and a government that remained staunchly neutral during the war, the Swiss were successful in making and selling Jockey shorts at home. Then with the war's end, Vollmoeller and Kneibler discussed and moved on to the next logical step, selling throughout Central Europe, where industrial production had been all but destroyed during the war and where any manufacturer who could turn out a product enjoyed a sure seller's market. With characteristic foresight and with Vollmoeller's help, Coopers formed ties with several more European manufacturers that made and sold Jockey according to designs established in Kenosha. Early license deals were struck in Germany and Scandinavia, where the market was eager to buy and where manufacturing standards in some cases exceeded those set by the American mill.

Coopers most indispensable contribution to their licensees came in merchandising and marketing. Within a few years, Jockey advertising was appearing in magazines and in outdoor advertising in many countries. Significantly, many of them made heavy use of English-language expressions to prove that Jockey products were American and thoroughly modern. "Jockey needed first to conquer the people who knew English and understood the American and English mentality," said Vollmoeller in Switzerland some years later. The growth of Jockey in Europe

suggested strongly that these markets were eager to adopt American customs and products.

Worldwide Brand

Jockey licensees grew in size and number in this period, not just in Europe but in South America as well. The latter market was developed primarily by Paul Baer, Coopers' multilingual director of licensing. Born in Germany and raised in Argentina, Baer was fluent in several languages and in the 1950s traveled widely in South America in search of good markets and likely licensees. Manufacturing, one of Coopers' greatest strengths, was a definite weakness in South America, where engineering and production talent was undeveloped and hard to find. Thus, Jockey presented itself as a good match in Argentina, Colombia, Peru and several other countries where licensing agreements were struck in the early and middle 1950s.

Here again, success required patience and an understanding of the local situation. While all of Latin America seemed to want Jockey products, the laws of many nations limited licensing agreements with broad restrictions on the exportation of currency. In some cases, the royalties that Coopers earned in South America could be transported to currency markets in Uruguay, where it was possible to buy dollars and bring them home to the U.S. In other cases, licensees paid royalties in the form of other locally produced merchandise, which Coopers sought to export, sell and convert into dollars.

These difficulties fell to a new generation of Coopers management, led by Robert

Cooper, who succeeded his father, Ralph, as president in 1957, and Jack Wyss, who became marketing vice president in 1956. Before long, they had mastered these foreign markets, with Wyss in particular traveling extensively to promote Jockey worldwide. Wyss was encouraged on these trips when he discovered that most people outside the U.S. were fascinated by all things American. "There is a wonderful opportunity for American industry in these areas, particularly for those firms with name-brand products," Wyss told the *Kenosha News* after one of his trips. "Maybe it's because the people [abroad] feel that any product which has survived the rigors of competition in the United States and has emerged a leader is the one they want."

This meant the Jockey brand, naturally, and by 1961, Wyss had hired a young German-raised marketing man, Ernie Ott, to expand the potential of the overseas market. Ott found that the European market was larger than anyone realized, and he soon suggested that Coopers was, if anything, too conservative in its approach. Early on, for example, Ott convinced senior management to allow the German and French licensees the freedom to produce briefs with a lower, more modern-looking rise. This was the first time anyone ever proposed altering the classic Jockey brief, and when Wyss permitted it, he told Ott, "You'd better be right or your head will roll." He was half-joking, but Ott turned out to be entirely right. The briefer brief was a big seller in Europe, where the Jockey name came to represent not just an American brand but a fashionable one as well.

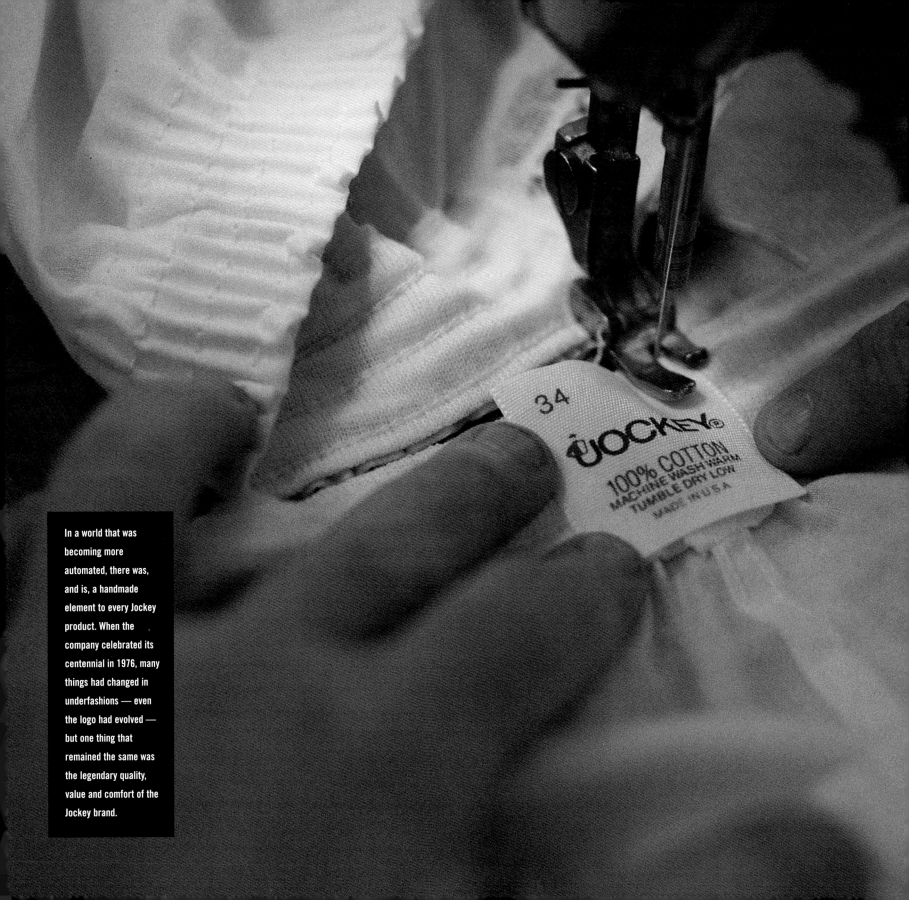

In a world that was becoming more automated, there was, and is, a handmade element to every Jockey product. When the company celebrated its centennial in 1976, many things had changed in underfashions — even the logo had evolved — but one thing that remained the same was the legendary quality, value and comfort of the Jockey brand.

Tradition Stays in Fashion

The Coopers sales force grew in size and sophistication in the booming postwar economy, but it never lost its grassroots character. No one knew the menswear and department stores of America quite like the Coopermen. They were a proud army, and as their numbers grew to more than 200 in the 1960s, they were on the road not just selling underwear but also looking for fresh talent to join them and make the company even stronger.

In 1952, for example, Jockey salesman Buck Rogers had his eye on a young retail clerk at Fischer's Men's Store in Fairmont, Minnesota, named Howie Ness. Rogers thought Ness would make a good Cooperman, but haberdasher Lee Fischer was Rogers's loyal customer and Ness was Fischer's best salesman. So Rogers never approached Ness — until the youngster quit Fischer's and made plans to take a new job in New Jersey. Only then did Rogers invite Ness to Kenosha for an interview. "I thought you'd never ask," said Ness, who went on to have a long and productive career as a Cooperman. There were many other such stories of good retail salesmen recruited to sell the brand that they knew was the best in the store.

Coopers, Inc., was known for its innovative products, but behind every new underwear style was a promise of reliable quality and timely delivery that was second to none in the fashion industry. Communications between the sales force, the office and production were key and were encouraged by the *Cooperator*, opposite, a newsletter in the 1940s and 1950s, covering all aspects of the business, including the Jockey-Coopers bowling team, a short-lived but famous pro squad that sometimes rolled against skilled amateurs from the office and plant.

But it wasn't just the customers who were eccentric. There was Cooperman Harold Boylan, for example, who handled the working-class South Side of Chicago where he exercised tough love on customers whether they were in a buying mood or not. Boylan was never slow to insult a buyer for carrying competitive brands, nor to offer his opinion of a store that did not carry a full line of Jockey underwear. Boylan sometimes demonstrated his technique in role-playing sessions at sales meetings. And while he softened his attack on these occasions, one colleague couldn't help but ask during one such presentation, "Now, Harold, how would you do that *without* your knee on the buyer's chest?"

Another Jockey original was Al Levin, who had a particular fondness for the Jockey Overknee, because, he insisted, they were highly useful in keeping the press in a pair of trousers. To prove this theory, Levin had a special pair of shorts constructed, with one leg of Midway length, the other Overknee. He wore them on sales calls where he provided incontrovertible evidence that the crease in the pant leg with the Overknee really did seem crisper. The result was that Levin's South Florida territory experienced excellent sales in the Overknee at a time when the product was regarded as antiquated in many other parts of the country.

Selling With the Personal Touch

These were the good old days for many Coopermen. Personal relationships with stores and buyers were key, a lesson that was pounded in early and often to new salesmen in small, often rural, "training territories." Salesman Mac Millholland, who later became manager of customer service in Kenosha, started his selling career in northern Indiana, where many stores had tin ceilings and pot-belly stoves. Millholland remembered one customer who always, without fail, had more hosiery in stock than there were feet in his county. But when Millholland arrived there was always one thing that he wanted to see first: hosiery.

Heading South

Overknees did finally go out of fashion, but Coopers was ready for change. Indeed, the company was well prepared for the future, due largely to the foresight of Harry Wolf Sr., who began his steady accumulation of Coopers stock in the 1940s. By the late 1950s, Wolf owned shares in Coopers roughly equal to those of Gib Lance. Then upon the death of Lance in 1960, Wolf acquired that stock from Gib's widow, Carlotta Cooper Lance — this in accordance with an agreement formed when both partners were alive.

Coopers was now owned nearly outright by Harry Wolf, a genius with numbers who amazed young bookkeepers with his swift command of the business during his visits to Kenosha, which came weekly and sometimes less frequently than that. Beyond the numbers, Wolf was also a management consultant with a sure grasp of long-term trends. It was Wolf, for example, who insisted that Jockey maintain its premium name with fair trade prices. He also organized time-and-motion studies on the factory floor and introduced incentive pay plans for the most loyal work force in Kenosha. Now, his understanding of another long-term trend — the increase of Northern labor and transportation costs — was behind his decision to shift an increasing portion of Coopers' manufacturing south of the Mason-Dixon line.

Wolf's first significant move in this direction came in 1948 when merchandising man Jim Drago, was searching for a new mill to make woven boxer shorts. Drago was having problems at the time with a small contract manufacturer in Paris, Kentucky, and after a little looking, he found another mill also in Kentucky to take up the slack. This was Giffin Manufacturing, in the town of Carlisle, run by three ex-employees of the Paris mill. Coopers became one of Giffin's first customers.

It was the beginning of a long relationship between Jockey and Giffin, owned by salesman Lonnie Giffin, floor supervisor Carrie Shumate, and machinist Clifford Shumate, Carrie's husband. Harry Wolf liked this hard-working group immensely, and shortly after that first contract, he made a minority investment in Giffin to give them a lift and give Coopers a lock on its production.

While the Giffin contract proved beneficial to all concerned, Coopers brought other Southern plants on line and bought them outright. In 1951, Coopers opened a mill in Millen, Georgia, where workers cut fabric, sewed Jockey shorts and undershirts, and packaged them for distribution. In 1956, they opened another in Belzoni, Mississippi, that did all that in addition to knitting the cotton into fabric at the front end of the process. These were highly efficient plants, equipped with modern machines and set up by engineering consultants Kurt Salmon Associates. While technical sophistication in these plants was important, they were by and large labor-intensive operations, and the element of human management was critical. A keen judge of management talent, Wolf sent individuals such as Fred Holmes, later vice president of manufacturing, to Georgia and Mississippi to train and streamline a process that cut and assembled more than a dozen separate pieces that constituted the Jockey brief.

These factories changed as the industry changed. The Millen operation finally left the old mill where it began and built a modern facility on the edge of town. In Kentucky, Wolf made additional investments in the Giffin mills until he acquired control of the business in 1964. In the decade that followed, Blue Grass Industries, as it was renamed, grew into an integrated network of five plants, all within 50 miles of one another, each involved in all or part of the manufacturing process from knitting, to sewing, to packaging the full line of Jockey underwear.

New Media Image

By the late 1950s, the Jockey line enjoyed a position of substantial strength — as strong as any apparel brand of its era. Coopers built this advantage through manufacturing know-how, a first-rate sales force and advertising at a high level. By now, advertising was particularly important, and with an ad budget of $1 million per year, the company's sense of image building was strong enough to survive and even benefit from its first frankly bizarre experience with television. What became known as the "Jack Parr fiasco" occurred in 1958, when Jockey purchased a series of 30-second live segments on the *Tonight Show*, at $5,000 each. This campaign was eagerly, perhaps nervously, anticipated by everyone in the company. President Bob Cooper was in the studio audience at Rockefeller Center the night of the first spot. Most of the rest of senior management gathered around Jack Wyss's television in Kenosha.

What happened could hardly have been predicted. Host Jack Parr no sooner pulled out the Jockey package and began reading the ad copy than he was struck by the strange notion of showing men's briefs on television. A few seconds later it struck him as very funny, and the best joke of the night was on its way. Parr was nearly doubled over by the time the 30-seconds were up, and with his sure knack for a good joke, he continued the commercial, laughing uncontrollably, holding up the package for the camera, and gasping the name "Jockey." It went on for more than two minutes, the longest two minutes a mortified Bob Cooper had ever experienced.

Nor was Jack Wyss thrilled as he watched in Kenosha. "They won't embarrass us like that twice," he said, and the next morning he canceled the rest of the *Tonight Show* contract. That was until they began getting reports from the stores. People loved the ad, and it was especially great, they said, that Jockey could poke fun at itself. So the spots continued on the *Tonight Show*, although Jack Parr never quite got used to them. Every Jockey commercial had the suspense of a quiz show, as least for Coopers management when they turned on the television to watch. Would Parr lose it? Not always, but one commercial was scheduled during a guest appearance by funnyman Jerry Lewis, who grabbed the package, opened it and pulled a pair of briefs on his head like a cap.

New Style for a New Era

Despite the steady and sometimes stupendous growth of Jockey shorts in the 1950s, management was well aware that a flow of fresh ideas was essential to the company's continued success. Even in the postwar heyday, Coopers

Jack Parr, one of the mega-celebrities of the 1950s, provided Jockey with mega-exposure on the *Tonight Show* when he pulled a package of Jockey shorts from behind his desk and prepared to read advertising copy. It always cracked him up, so that each television spot carried a bit of suspense. Would he get through the live commercial or not?

introduced a number of specialty items — boxer shorts with big red hearts for Valentine's Day, and animal-skin prints that sold best around Father's Day. Designer underwear was a stretch for most retailers, but management felt best when they were generating new ideas. The sales force enjoyed the break from selling "tighty whiteys" too.

While never interrupting the classic-brief juggernaut, other introductions included Jockey Skants, a low-cut, rayon-knit brief that

was thoroughly modern and proved that European styling was already influencing merchandisers in Kenosha. Introduced in 1958, Skants represented an early nod to the inevitable fact that a new generation of Jockey wearers was on the rise. They grew up in Jockey briefs and appeared loyal, but a variation on the traditional theme, they thought, might give the whole line more luster. Skants went on to enjoy substantial success among a growing market of American males who were

Life in men's underwear was never like this! But by the 1970s, Jockey Life helped make it the era of self-expression. Comedian Wally Cox was an early TV spokesman for this colorful product, and in commercials he shed his milquetoast persona whenever he had the bold colors and profiles of Jockey Life underneath. In 1973, screen star Godfrey Cambridge made a Jockey Life commercial and asked, "Whoever said underwear has to be white, anyhow? People come in colors don't they?"

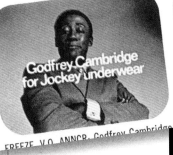

Godfrey Cambridge for Jockey underwear

FREEZE V.O. ANNCR. Godfrey Cambridge

CAMBRIDGE (LIGHTS COME UP, HE

not squeamish about fashion.

Jockey's next major step in modernizing men's underwear came in 1965 with the introduction of Jockey Life, a line of bright hues, briefer cuts and various fabrics (some synthetic) again inspired by closer relations with Jockey licensees in Europe. Style-conscious French and color-loving Scandinavians had been wearing different styles of Jockey underwear for several years now — licensed products that always amused management in Kenosha when samples were sent across. Now, Jockey merchandisers believed, America was ready for a new line of briefs, boxers and undershirts that were designed to be seen. They were right. Jockey Life proved that American men (and the women who dressed them) were glad to spend a little more time and money on underwear.

Within just a few years, the Jockey Life line accounted for 25 percent of Coopers' business — happy proof that the company was still good at translating social trends. The advertising that promoted Jockey Life also proved that the firm hadn't lost their touch in that area either. Jockey Life enjoyed its first surge of public recognition with television commercials that exploited the not-so-subtle irony of selling "unmentionables" on the small screen. In one early campaign, comedian Wally Cox claimed that his normally timid persona was transformed when girded with the brash colors of Jockey Life underneath. A later commercial revived Jockey's old affinity with sports stars. The most endearing new twist on this old theme was with baseball star Yogi Berra and his three sons. Old Yogi wore Jockey white underwear and expressed

bemusement that his long-haired kids, standing around him and dressed in Jockey Life, went for colors.

None of these television spots showed men in underwear below the waist, which would have violated broadcasting standards at the time. For this reason, plus the fast-rising price of television time, Coopers management concluded that if Jockey Life was its message, print was its medium. By 1976 the vast majority of the company's ad budget of some $2 million was in magazines (and some in newspapers), where the company had the freedom to verge gently into territory that may have challenged the status quo but never overstepped what was recognized as good taste. National magazines such as *Sports Illustrated* and *Esquire*, among others, gave Coopers a place to show the world what management believed was new. That was colored, sometimes-revealing underwear, low in the waist, high in the hip. Names like Elance, Poco and Micro-3 broadened the image of the company, and some features, such as mesh fabrics, put Jockey underwear in a category that might have seemed unthinkable before this time.

Conquering a Fashionable World

Nobody at Coopers ever forgot that their staple product was still the classic brief. Yet the company's latest move into fashion underwear proved that the only constant in this industry, beside the basic Jockey short, was the necessity for change. Nobody saw this more clearly than Jack Wyss, the Kenosha boy who became president of the company in 1971. Wyss was raised in the Coopers tradition, which was a conservative family business that also depended on the constant embrace of innovation and fashion.

By the end of the 1960s, Jack Wyss saw the world changing more swiftly than it had ever changed before. A revolution in social customs — and new value placed on self-expression — opened new horizons in men's fashion, not only in underwear but in some lines of sportswear that Jockey decided to market as well. Expanded lines of sport shirts, slacks, shorts and sweaters were a logical extension of the brand, thought Wyss and Wally Erickson, merchandising vice president. The sales force had been selling casual items like elasticized Ban-Lon shirts for several years and was still having success with a line of golf wear endorsed by Tony Lema before the golf star's untimely death.

As Wyss and his marketing department imagined a wider line of sportswear, they took the emphatic and positive step of changing the company name from Coopers, Inc., known mostly as an old-line underwear company, to Jockey Menswear in 1971, then in 1972 to Jockey International. The newly named company would use its famous trademark to make its mark in sportswear and "activewear" designed for athletics. In the early 1970s, for example, the company established a new line called Trophy, fashions for the golf course with endorsers Bert Yancy and Tom Weiskopf doing the modeling. A less likely innovation was something called DP, or "dual purpose," sportswear. The idea was "making undershorts into swim wear," as a trade magazine described Jockey's multicolored briefs that were suitable for both.

Sportswear had a significant impact on

In the 1970s, Jockey had some very good years in what they called "active wear," but when designer labels eclipsed the older brands in the 1990s, Jockey got out of sportswear.

Jockey's bottom line, and by 1975 accounted for one-third of the company's sales. Not every product was a long-term success, naturally. Double-knit slacks and leisure suits had their run, especially in the Corn Belt. "Easterners called us the leisure suit capital of the world," said Ed Gill, then a salesman based in Omaha. But even here, Jockey sportswear lived, died and sometimes stumbled on short-lived trends. Gill remembered that he did fine with navy blue double-knits for a year or two, but he could only shake his head when the yellows and pinks were still in the stores and waiting for customers a year or more after they came out.

Sportswear and activewear kept changing, and Jockey worked hard to stay abreast of trends that drove the industry's fickle fates. Tennis — as a sport and as a fashion statement — experienced a big bulge in the 1980s, for example, and the clothes that McEnroe and Bjorg wore became popular for people who never held a racquet. Jockey's sportswear vice president, Rick Hosley, started referring to tennis shorts and warm-up suits as "mowing-the-lawn-wear," and the market grew large enough to sign advertising and endorsement contracts with ranked players like Harold Solomon and Brad Gilbert.

Jockey tennis wear never quite took off, and the category eventually became dominated by America's shoe manufacturers, such as Nike. Eventually, the whole sportswear market began to trail off, a trend typified by an incident in the mid-1980s when a thief broke into the showroom during a sales meeting in Florida. The perpetrator stole all the underwear he or she could carry off but left the sportswear behind — a message that management couldn't help but notice. But when Jockey left sportswear altogether in the early 1990s, the business had left some permanent positive effects. One was that the company had forged closer relations with licensees, some of whom continued as sportswear fashion leaders in Europe. Sportswear also created new bonds with offshore manufacturers, who produced much of this merchandise. The American tennis boom would shrink, but it had helped establish Jockey on an increasingly international court.

Strengthening the Family Spirit

As Jockey broadened and grew, the importance of its tightly knit, family-style traditions were challenged, but they were never let go. President Jack Wyss retired in 1975 and was replaced by longtime Cooperman Dick Jensen, who had been the regional vice president of sales in California. Jensen reflected the family spirit that had served the company for 99 years; he was born and raised in Kenosha and had been a part of the company since the mid-1930s, when he was hired to model the new classic brief. Jensen's handsome physique represented the first introduction of Jockey to a generation of consumers.

Despite its happy ties with the past, the company was not without its stresses and strains. Harry Wolf Sr., who had owned and guided the company for more than three decades, was now retiring from active control. In his place his son, Harry Jr., known as Buddy, became chairman in 1976. Also in a position of considerable power, as chairman of the executive committee, was Wayne

Shumate of Blue Grass Industries, whose parents were Harry Sr.'s early partners in the Kentucky mills. While Shumate brought a high level of manufacturing expertise to the company, he could only watch as the financial and marketing control began to unravel; many longtime executives could see that the company was in a slow but dangerous downward spiral.

Whatever outside forces influenced the company's performance during that time, the chairmanship of Buddy Wolf marked a period when Jockey simply lost its cutting-edge dominance in the market. That, combined with growing management expenses, spelled difficulty. Particularly attuned to these threats were Jensen, Wally Erickson and Financial Vice President Paul Sebastian, all of whom assisted in a move to bring Harry Wolf's two daughters, Donna Wolf Steigerwaldt and Mary Bogue, onto the Jockey board. This occurred over the vehement protests of Buddy, but what amounted to a changing of the guard was completed in 1978 when Steigerwaldt became chairman of the company.

The coming of Donna Wolf Steigerwaldt was the beginning of a new golden age at Jockey. While the transition from Buddy to Donna was protracted and sometimes stormy, there was a strong feeling in the Kenosha office that Donna would bring a new sense of openness and enthusiasm to the company. She quickly brought expenses under control and as full-time chairman and CEO established quick rapport with senior staff. She even brought back executives such as Ernie Ott as president of the international division after he

left in the wake of disagreements with the previous leadership.

Steigerwaldt also met frequently with employees at large and left everyone with the feeling that this was now a family company again. She admitted freely that she had been out of the workplace for more than 20 years (she had worked in the insurance business after college) but that she was back because she cared about preserving something that was all too rare in corporate America — a business where success was not measured solely in quarterly results. Very quickly, she became known as a "people person," treating her staff with respect and talking to plant personnel as colleagues and friends.

From the beginning, she was strikingly open about her hopes for the company and her concerns. When a national magazine listed her as one of the most important female CEOs in the country, she was quoted as saying that her father "never even considered having his daughters in the business with him." But when asked what was important to her, she told another interviewer that "I'd like the people of Jockey to know that it was me who carried on the tradition."

That tradition involved Jockey's well-known strengths, such as its reputation for quality and innovation, and reviving a once sparkling brand name in men's apparel. At the same time, she was blazing her own trail in what had been a male-dominated company. She succeeded in both, and when she brought the company back to its profitable glow, she also ushered in a new age not just for Jockey but for the entire underwear industry.

Among the many turning points in Jockey history, Donna Wolf Steigerwaldt's taking the reins as chairman and CEO was of major importance. Before Donna, the company was foundering on past laurels. With Donna, the company's most important tradition was its knack for innovation. Best of all, Donna Steigerwaldt knew the difference between a flash in the pan and real fashion, such as Jockey for Her Elance, opposite, introduced in 1987.

The Glamorous New World

From the moment Donna Wolf Steigerwaldt introduced herself to the employees at Kenosha, she instilled confidence from top to bottom. She said she was intent on maintaining Jockey as a family company. This referred to its ownership, which was private, and the management style, which was based on trust.

"She had the ability to bring people together and let them do their job," said Paul Sebastian, vice president of finance and Donna's close confidant as she learned about the company's financial position. For the people working at Jockey, her willingness to "let people be their own bosses," as she described her management style, was a breath of fresh air. On the outside, the people who did business with Jockey saw something of the old days under her father. Banks that had resisted big commitments a few years earlier were now competing to do business with Jockey.

Donna brought stability back to Jockey, although her earliest decisions also suggested that she was willing to make changes. Change

Howard Cooley was named president of Jockey International in 1979. He had been a principal with Kurt Salmon Associates, the consultants that Donna Steigerwaldt hired to survey and help revive the company when she became chairman. When Cooley said that the company needed a new president, Donna said it would be a short search — the best candidate was already in the room.

president from the outside to spark new energy and innovation. And as conversations focused on who that person should be, it wasn't long before they focused on someone already in the room — Cooley himself.

Innovation with Tradition

This was the beginning of an excellent collaboration between Steigerwaldt and Cooley, both of whom had a deep respect for tradition and a sharp eye for the newest opportunities in the business.

Indeed, within a few years, the Steigerwaldt-Cooley leadership generated some of the company's greatest marketing triumphs ever. But before the new products and new campaigns, they focused on something less flashy, engineering and production. Textile engineering was Cooley's métier, and among his first moves when he became president in 1979 was the launch of two Jockey-owned spinning mills, the first in Cedar Falls, North Carolina, and the second in nearby Abbeville.

Vertical integration was the modern term for manufacturing from fiber to finished product; and now it reflected that Jockey had the size and power of a major apparel company. There was, however, an aspect of the new trend at Jockey that harked directly back to the years when the Cooper brothers themselves handled everything from spinning to selling. When they opened Cedar Falls in 1981, it paralleled 1879 when old Reverend Cooper rehired the work force of a knitting mill that had burned down. Jockey did something similar, purchasing an abandoned yarn factory, modernizing the machinery, and

began in earnest when she called in the consultants at Kurt Salmon Associates to revamp an organization in need of direction. Kurt Salmon had a history with Jockey, having assisted in launching the Southern plants. Now they sent one of their principals to Kenosha — Howard Cooley, who knew Jockey since the 1960s and understood better than anyone that it remained a golden name in the apparel business. While Donna was often distressed at the financial situation she

found when she arrived, Cooley could soothe her fears. "You couldn't kill this company with a stick," he said. He assured her that good overall leadership would return it to its former glory.

What Cooley saw was a company with loyal employees, strong managers and an untarnished image in the marketplace. As a consultant, Cooley also agreed with Steigerwaldt and senior executives Jensen and Sebastian that the company needed a new

Under Cooley, the company became vertically integrated — manufacturing its own yarn and opening new plants in North Carolina, Jamaica and points south. As Jockey became more efficient, its designs became more stylish as well. Here an employee oversees the dying process in the 1980s when color was one of the keynotes of the new Jockey.

Jockey's chic Elance was sold in clear tubes, three pairs to the tube, a package that stressed the brevity of the style and the brightness of its colors.

approach was embodied by Leyendecker's "Man on the Bag." Later, Jockey underwear was endorsed by athletes like golfer Tommy Armour and quarterback Sammy Baugh. For years, the company had displayed a genius for attention-getting advertising that didn't draw undue attention to the fact that underwear was anatomically explicit.

Effective image building was not simple, however. Like the products they promoted, each new Jockey campaign inched into territory where polite advertising had not inched before. By the 1970s, social mores were changing more quickly than ever, and advertising, too, was being pushed beyond what was conventional. Jockey moved courageously beyond the longtime keynotes of comfort and fit, and now promoted itself with a measure of sex appeal too.

Jockey's best answer to the fragile business of male sex appeal was essentially a return, in 1976, to the tried and true. Jockey released a print ad featuring a page of eight famous, half-dressed jocks. "Take off their uniforms and who are they?" was the clever slogan. The answer was that they were normal guys who liked colorful skivs, which was an ingenious and not-too-subtle way to erase any doubts about fashionable underwear.

This sports-hero campaign was effective and ran for more than a year. It sold plenty of underwear, but it did something else that was even more important. It brought Jim Palmer, future Hall of Fame pitcher, to Jockey, where he became one of the best-known product spokesmen in America. Discovering just how good Palmer would be happened largely by accident. This was after Jockey's ad agency

sending manager Jim Andreucci from Kenosha to rehire the men and women who used to work there.

Marketing for a New Generation

Marketing and advertising, too, was revitalized, though it was still based on the old Jockey idea that quality underwear could and should be celebrated. Years before, this snagged an invitation from the daytime *Mike Douglas Show*, which agreed to a men's underwear fashion show, with another Jockey model, Pete Rose, appearing (fully clothed) to discuss the subject on the air. But at the last moment Rose canceled, and the show's producers were about to scrub the whole idea when advertising manager Bill Hermann got on the phone to Jim Palmer. Palmer, who was also in the "Take Off Their Uniforms" ad, gladly agreed to drive from Baltimore, where he lived, to Philadelphia, where the program was produced, and talk about modeling underwear.

It was an early and happy chapter of a long relationship between Palmer and Jockey. Actually, Palmer was a dream from the beginning. It was he who had shown the most willingness — the least self-consciousness — to model Elance, the briefest and most provocative of the Jockey fashion line, in the "Take Off Their Uniforms" ad. After *Mike Douglas*, it wasn't long before Palmer was appearing by himself in a new series of Jockey ads. They hardly broke new ground in male nudity, but the pitcher's fame and scant cladding raised

Whatever risks Jockey took in picturing Baltimore Orioles hurler Jim Palmer in his underwear reaped major league results. Partially clothed males were not at all usual in American advertising at the time, and the press had a field day with Jim Palmer's latest pitch.

eyebrows and drew the attention of men who otherwise paid little attention to what was new in men's underwear.

By 1980, the Palmer campaign was widely considered a success, and advertising veteran Bill Hermann was promoted to advertising vice president. Hermann had been saying for a long time that what Jockey needed was more of Jim Palmer, not just in print ads, but on billboards, in personal appearances and as the personality who would become inextricably linked with Jockey.

So it was that in late summer of that year, Palmer was on a huge billboard over Times Square in New York City and was attending press conferences on Jockey's behalf, all of which received positive notices that did not neglect the gentle irony that accompanied Palmer's latest "pitch." Within a few months, it was obvious that Jim Palmer was the perfect messenger to tell the world that men in fashionable underwear were okay. Fan mail started coming in — no matter that most was from women. "I've been a Los Angeles Dodger fan most of my life," wrote one. "But I just picked up a magazine and saw your picture in it. That's enough to make any girl switch teams and leagues, and that's just what I've done."

Palmer handled the adulation with poise and charm. During an appearance at a department store, a young woman asked him to autograph the underwear that she was wearing. He obliged and was quite willing to linger in this task. "Would you like my middle name too?" he asked.

For Her

Palmer's popularity with women (who still purchased 65 percent of the men's underwear sold) as well as men moved Jockey closer, perhaps unconsciously, to a product line that seemed out of bounds at first. It came at a time when the Jockey brand was acquiring not just respect but glamour. It also came when new efficiency in manufacturing — a consequence of new leadership — led to overcapacity. The move was also determined, at least in part, by the definite trend toward androgyny in women's fashions. The latest innovation — perhaps the most radical ever at Jockey — was women's underwear.

To some, "Jockey for Her" looked like a disaster waiting to happen. Hardly any other brand in America had quite the masculinized image that Jockey did. And cotton panties represented a minuscule percentage of women's underfashions at the time. Add to this Jockey's previous experiment in women's underwear, Jockette, in 1952, and there were plenty of reasons to think of Jockey shorts for women as someone's bad joke.

Donna Steigerwaldt did not agree, of course. She sensed that women appreciated the comfort of cotton. She also believed that what women's underwear often lacked the kind of quality that had made Jockey famous. Perhaps most important of all, Donna had the instinct to reconsider an idea that others condemned because it failed 30 years before. Cooley was in full agreement — he was also eager to make use of excess production capacity — and Jockey for Her was introduced in 1982.

It was anything but an impulsive move, of course. With research coordinated by Don Ruland and Debra Steigerwaldt Waller, Donna Steigerwaldt's daughter, they made prototypes and gave them to Carthage College students and a group of Chicago-based flight attendants. Reports back were positive; someone in the company (perhaps a former dissenter) even produced a file of letters from women who bought and wore men's Elance bikinis because they liked the fit and the fashion of Jockey underwear.

A Roaring Start

Jockey for Her began with a product line of three styles — a full-coverage brief, middle-coverage hipster and bikini — each one in four different colors. The company planned to introduce the new line at a high-impact fashion show with Jim Palmer as host and master of ceremonies. Though the event took place at the tony New York Athletic Club during a major apparel market then taking place in the city, Jockey executives were plenty nervous about getting a crowd big enough to match their hopes for the new line.

The morning of the show, salesmen were passing out invitations to anyone and every-one they could find to make sure the room was full.

As it turned out, conventioneers came in droves, and so did the trade and local press. No one was bored, certainly, when the run-way show opened with the "history of under-wear," going back to the skins that cavemen and cavewomen must have worn for warmth if not cleanliness. The story quickly leapt for-ward to the Coopers era of union suits, nain-sooks and finally Y-Front briefs. As the music grew louder, the men's fashion era was marched out, and then, after great suspense, came the women.

When the smoke had cleared, Jockey had impressed the trade and had even made it onto most of the airwaves of New York. Indeed, Jockey for Her's introduction was a stunning success, and the only ones displeased were the staid management of the New York Athletic Club. They shot off a letter to Jockey's PR agent, Erica Feinberg, claiming that they had been deceived into hosting a strip show and that Jockey wouldn't darken their hallowed halls again.

Jockey for Her next made its way into

Jockey for Her caught many trends at the perfect moment. Women, many of whom had been buying men's Elance for its all-cotton comfort, quickly converted to Jockey for Her after its introduction in 1982. Despite the eventual triumph of Jockey for Her, there was trepidation beforehand, as Jockey old-timers remembered the less than successful Jockette, from 1952, opposite.

test markets where results were equally encouraging. In Milwaukee, for example, President Cooley and Executive Vice President Wally Erickson met to discuss the new line with Gimbel's executives, including store president Tom Grimes. Halfway through the presentation, Grimes interrupted. "You don't have to sell me," he said. "Let's write an order right now." Jockey wasn't quite ready for such enthusiasm; they hadn't even settled on retail prices for the line.

Not everyone was quite so ready and willing. In New York, one big retailer couldn't get over the fact that Jockey for Her was sold in polyethylene wrappers, not on hangers, which were standard for women's underwear. "Who'd buy underwear like that?" asked the buyer. "It looks just like men's." But in just a few weeks, Jockey for Her was a big hit across town at Bloomingdale's, and the reluctant retailer quickly placed an order.

Across the nation, the public responded. Many women got their first pair in a tremendously successful promotion with coupons good for a free pair of Jockey for Her. The company printed a million of these, and salesmen passed them out to everyone they met. Retail saleswomen got them, tried them and became big promoters of Jockey for Her. Books of coupons also went to every gynecologist in America, a successful promotion followed by a spate of publicity that breathable cotton was more hygienic than synthetic fabric was. The latter was a talking point that reminded old-timers of urologists in the 1930s who endorsed masculinized Jockeys for their healthful qualities.

These were particularly good days for the sales force, and any fear that senior salesmen would balk at selling Jockey for Her proved unfounded. A few had trouble getting in to see intimate wear buyers at first, but when they did, longtime Coopermen became the cotton panty's biggest promoters anywhere. Howie Ness, then in his 60s, handed out coupons en masse to flight attendants; they loved cotton Jockey for Her and never forgot Ness when they met him again. "After Jockey for Her, I don't think I ever paid for a drink on an airplane," Ness joked after he retired a few years later.

Designed for Women

In a period of changing roles for women, Jockey was on the front lines, it appeared, to champion the cause. Donna Steigerwaldt appeared on the *Oprah Winfrey Show*, where Oprah was fascinated by many things about the Jockey CEO, not least of all that a woman could run a men's underwear company, then create a successful line for women as well. A short time later, feminist author Susan Faludi applauded Jockey in her book *Backlash*, where she claimed that Jockey was one of the few companies that actually consulted and listened to women when designing underwear for them.

Most important to the success of Jockey for Her was its "real-woman" campaign launched shortly after the line was introduced. "Look who's wearing Jockey now" was the tag line accompanied by career women, many working in formerly male-dominated professions. The women were dressed in their work clothes, which also revealed their cotton Jockey for Her underwear. The ads featured various professions. A woman physician naturally reinforced the health message, but other ads included a policewoman and a number of business executives.

As the "real-woman" ads blitzed the women's magazines, the campaign had an important unintended effect — women who wrote in by the dozens to offer their services for the ads. Whatever motivated them, it seemed partly due to a deep-down desire of some American women to pose in their underwear. This, it appeared, represented something other than unalloyed feminism, and within a year of the launch of the campaign, Jockey for Her kicked up enough ideological dust to merit a good-natured debate on the *Today* show.

Opposed to the campaign was syndicated columnist Ellen Goodman. "There are too many who still see a sex object under every success suit," Goodman later wrote in a column. She suggested that chauvinists, consciously or not, were co-opting feminists. Taking the other side of the question, Howard Cooley was joined by Jeanie Zadrozny, a Pittsburgh business consultant and recent Jockey model. Cooley didn't say much. He didn't have to, because Zadrozny insisted that she was pleased to be admired for her physical assets as well as her professional ones and that appearing in a Jockey ad wasn't bad for business either. Cooley only nodded at a point well made and even joked that host Jane Pauley might like to try out for an ad herself.

Sharing Success

Jockey had become a new company under Donna Steigerwaldt, who instilled confidence

"Look Who's Wearing Jockey Now" was the campaign that featured Jockey's satisfied customers. In this ad from 1985, model Rebecca Machan with her daughter Tessa shows how comfortable women can be in their underwear. This ad series was cited by Women Against Pornography, a national group active against provocative images of women that were flooding the media at the time.

JOCKEY *For Her*

Look who's wearing Jockey now.

She's comfortable with loving.
She has magic in her eyes.

Flowers bloom for her. White caps dance for her. A baby cries and laughs for her.

She's **Rebecca Machan**. Top fashion model, needlepoint artist, weekend camper, loving mother.

Jockey for Her full brief with camisole is made to fit her. Comfortable, durable, feminine, in absorbent 100% soft, combed cotton. So lightweight, it breathes. With no show leg and waistband. In her favorite colors. Also available in bikini and hipster styles.

A COMMITMENT TO QUALITY AND VALUE.
UNDERWEAR • SPORTSWEAR • HOSIERY • SLEEPWEAR

Rebecca Machan: Zoli Management Inc., New York   © 1984 Jockey International Inc., Kenosha, WI 53140.

company's social events and even dressing up for theme picnics, like Roaring Twenties Day at Millen where she dressed as a flapper. She also liked to exchange recipes with employees, and this went beyond casual banter when she joined a group of workers at Cedar Falls in putting out a Jockey cookbook.

This kind of management style paid off, because Steigerwaldt's employees discussed more than burgoo stew with their CEO. When the air conditioning at one plant began to fail, Steigerwaldt heard about it early and fixed it right away. In another plant, when parts of certain garments were not fitting together as well as they should, Steigerwaldt didn't take long to find a solution to improve the fabric cutting technology. Changes like these were made not through muttered complaints and slow half-measures, but by swift executive action. In 1988, the Randleman plant manager said he wanted to hire Mrs. Steigerwaldt as personnel manager — she had that much rapport with the employees. She had to decline, she said, because she was otherwise occupied.

Even the cynics were caught off guard by Donna Steigerwaldt's sincerity. One day in 1991 she called all employees working at Kenosha for a meeting in the cafeteria. Showing all the emotion she felt, Donna expressed gratitude for results that continued on an upward climb. Productivity was way up. Profits, especially from Jockey for Her, were beyond anyone's expectations. As she fought back tears, futilely for the most part, she announced that the Christmas bonus would be doubled and would continue at that level as long as the company could afford it.

in everyone who worked for her. While this applied to senior staff and managers, Steigerwaldt had almost uncanny rapport with the rank and file workforce as well. From the beginning of her chairmanship, she said she wanted to get to know her employees personally. She proved it by walking through the factory floor at Kenosha and in the Southern

plants and talking to people about their jobs and their lives.

"She really is a warm and friendly person," said one sewing machine operator to a reporter from a national magazine. "She really seems to care about what you have to say." Her hands-on management style had her joining in with the rest of the employees at the

Most steps in the manufacturing process have been modernized and computerized at Jockey facilities in the U.S. and overseas, but the human touch has never been lost. Here, a Jockey employee monitors the consistency of cotton yarn for any imperfection that might compromise product quality.

New Manufacturing Benchmarks

Success at Jockey required more than good-will and well-fitted underwear. It required a precise response to constant changes in the textile industry, which was the kind of moving target that Jockey became good at tracking and responding to.

As apparel manufacturing remained labor intensive, it was essential to implement labor-saving techniques whenever and wherever possible. Cooley ordered the installation of automatic cutting machines that used a kind of die-cut technology to stamp out dozens of pieces of fabric in a single punch. These machines improved speed and precision as never before, and the Millen plant, managed by Joe Burke, became a kind of showplace and laboratory for the Italian manufacturer of the cutting machines. Other technologies were less revolutionary, perhaps, but just as useful; among them were "gadgets," as they were called by the piecework employees, that guided the sewing of waistbands and leg elastic, parts of Jockey shorts that used to require the steadiest hand in the sewing room to assemble without mishap.

These production improvements were particularly important by the middle 1980s when the explosive success of Jockey for Her made additional production capacity an urgent priority. Increased demand in this period led to many decisions that were unexpected at the time, such as a delay in plans to close down the old Kenosha mill. Some things had changed in Kenosha — a largely Italian workforce had become a veritable United Nations with workers from many countries, including a recent influx of highly motivated women from Southeast Asia. Sewing was also restarted at one of the old Blue Grass facilities in Kentucky that was previously closed during an earlier streamlining effort.

Rebuilding capacity in old facilities was a stopgap, of course. The real trend in textiles and apparel was then, as in the past, the southward migration of manufacturing. By the mid-1980s, the necessity for a new pool of labor had Howard Cooley traveling to Jamaica to find a site for what would become, once it was up and running, one of the company's more successful undertakings of the decade. On one of his initial trips to the island in 1986, Cooley identified the town of Lucea, on the north shore of the island, west of Montego Bay. There Jockey could fulfill its goal to be the leading and most desirable employer in whatever labor market it was in. When the Lucea plant opened the next year, Jockey pay outstripped other jobs in the area. The company instituted a private health care program for employees. Later that year, when Lucea and the surrounding area was devastated by the worst hurricane in decades, Jockey took the lead in helping the region clean up the damage and recover.

Lucea represented one link in a successful model for Jockey and companies like it. While the highly mechanized side of manufacturing continued in the U.S. — weaving the fabric in North Carolina and cutting it in Kentucky — the sewing and packaging was done most economically offshore. In the next eight years, Jockey built similar offshore sewing facilities in Sandy Bay, Jamaica; San Jose, Costa Rica; and San Pedro Sula, Honduras.

Change continued as sheer hosiery represented the next logical step for the company whose briefs and bikinis had won the hearts of women all over America. Starting in 1988, Jockey for Her pantyhose were manufactured in a Randleman, North Carolina, mill purchased from Nantucket Industries. After a slow start production-wise, Jockey succeeded by doing what it had done before — finding experienced managers who had worked in the mill before Jockey owned it. One such person was Charlie Lamb, who knew the automated knitting machines like he knew his own truck. As director of hosiery, Lamb helped raise production from 4,000 dozen per week to 25,000 dozen in his first few months on the Jockey payroll.

In the 1990s, change continued at a rapid pace, and not always on an upward trend. Randleman closed in the year 2000, for example, when contracts to produce hosiery for other companies, which was profitable business for the plant, went elsewhere. There were other, more difficult setbacks in the 1990s as the company faced economic shifts through streamlining and attempted economies of scale. They were signaled by economic shifts in the company and in the world economy. But the company encountered a rocky road.

In 1993, for example, new senior management came on, led by Tom Beinemann as new managing director. Recognizing the need for change, Beinemann initiated a series of new manufacturing and distribution standards, many of which were difficult for the company to assimilate. Among these changes, additional manufacturing was moved offshore, not only to Jockey-owned plants but to contract manufacturers the world over, an approach that was as difficult as it was indispensable.

Early on, the foreign sourcing of shorter-run fashion products led to unexpected problems when little-known factories failed to deliver. These troubles were combined in 1993 with the shift to a single distribution center to handle all deliveries for the United States and Canada. Ultimately, developing sourcing capabilities and concentrating distribution in Cooleemee, North Carolina, brought the level of efficiency that Tom Beinemann envisioned.

A New Roadmap for a New World

Challenging times in the mid-1990s would eventually lead to the next phase at Jockey, the presidency of Edward C. Emma, appointed in 1995. Emma had come to the company five years before to head another important innovation, the growing network of outlet stores. As a retailing professional who previously worked at Jordan Marsh as vice president of merchandising, Emma was well aware of Jockey's strengths. Decades of quality and innovation had built a loyal following, so loyal that many stores forgave delivery breakdowns that would have erased almost any other brand from the marketplace.

Under Emma, Jockey took aggressive steps to build back its most enduring asset, which was making, selling and delivering classic white underwear and the basic lines of Jockey for Her. Getting this end of the business on track first had a series of subsequent effects. For one, it instilled new confidence in the retailers, particularly the large department stores, where Jockey had long enjoyed a leading position. For another, it showed the employees inside the company that success was a methodical process and based first and foremost on reliability.

Once the classics were getting sold and delivered on time, Jockey revived its role as underwear's fashion-forward leader as well. Each new success along these lines, with new and sometimes surprising designs in both women's and men's fashion underwear, was more than just a financial success. Each one illustrated that the market was increasingly diverse, but could be mastered if each segment were studied individually. It was a new way of thinking, but it also represented a kind of customer-centered approach that harked back to Henry Cooper's Kenosha Klosed Krotch.

Now, of course, being customer-driven was more complicated than ever. "Consumers aren't in one big bowl," Emma said. "Different types of consumers think in different ways." The new president's job was to draw a new road map to reach them all.

Jockey was already one of the nation's most recognizable brand names when the company began opening outlet stores in the late 1970s. By the 1990s, they cast an increasingly chic image and functioned as a way to collect vital information — products and customers could be tracked and matched with precision — in a marketplace that was more fluid than ever.

Opportunities for the Millennium

Jockey International had mastered new products and markets for more than 100 years, but the 1990s presented challenges as never before — consolidation in the retail sector was one, emerging global markets was another. Facing those challenges, management kept one eye on change and the other firmly fixed on Jockey's core values, which were constant. Quality, comfort and fit remained key to Jockey's reputation. Innovation remained indispensable. Inside the company, the family-oriented management reinforced a reputation that was as indispensable as it was intangible.

In real terms, Donna Steigerwaldt's company remained strong. Jockey continued as the Cadillac of American underwear. Its sales force was second to none. Its manufacturing personnel were skilled and loyal. And management was asking the right questions at the right time: How could a classic like Jockey flourish in a fashion-mad world? What sacrifices were needed to make the company thoroughly up-to-date?

New Markets in View

One major change came in the late 1980s, with the phenomenal growth of discount chains, which were attracting underwear buyers, among others, who used to shop at department stores like Marshall Field's and Macy's. K-Mart and Wal-Mart were changing the retail landscape, and while Jockey didn't sell through them, they were growing altogether too big to ignore.

Jockey's earliest response to the discount phenomenon came when it entered discussions with J. C. Penney in 1988. Penney's, a longtime national chain, was moving up-market and recasting its image to rise above the price-slashing fray. Penney's represented an enormous opportunity for Jockey, but also a fragile one. On the one hand, Penney's had 1,300 stores; on the other, doing business with Penney's could cause problems with established customers.

With eyes wide open, Vice President Wally Erickson and salesman Peter Hannes negotiated with Penney's and agreed to something new: a full line of men's underwear with a new trademark, in this case Thorobred. Penney's introduced the line in 1990, and it was so successful so quickly that the store asked to take the next step in 1991, which was to sell the Jockey line and place a name synonymous with distinction in what used to be a discount store. Inside Jockey, opinions

were split, but Donna Steigerwaldt concluded, like her successful predecessors, that change was the lifeblood of the business. She sold to Penney's, and she was right. Within another year, the account logged a sales surge that old-timers at Jockey compared to the invention of the original Jockey brief.

This success opened the door to new opportunities along similar lines — doing business with other proprietary brand names. Again, it was a successful shift; special markets of this kind became one of Jockey's fastest growing segments in the 1990s. This strategy was not universally endorsed inside the company. Some believed that new labels diluted the strength of the Jockey name and trademark. But most admitted that the new sales channels were here to stay. "You can't be

all things to all people," said Peter Hannes, who headed the special markets division, later named Thorobred Brands.

Later in the 1990s, as discount chains were taking in 40 percent of all men's underwear dollars, Hannes's view prevailed, not only at Jockey but in the stores as well. There, premium-quality products — new Jockey labels like Life in Wal-Mart and Form Fit in Target — found a prominent place alongside value-price merchandise.

The Outlet Explosion

While Jockey developed private brands for big retail chains, consumers were making another change in buying habits — the 1990s became a decade for the outlet store. The concept of a Jockey outlet actually went back to 1978 and the company's first "factory store" in Kenosha. With big discounts on second-quality and outdated merchandise, it garnered a big public following, and it was also considered risky business, since nearby retailers cried, perhaps exaggerating, that it cut deep into their markets.

But outlet malls sprung up around the country and were here to stay by the late

1980s. Initially, they carefully avoided competition with established retailers; most malls were outside metro areas, and Jockey opened stores in places like a center on I-94 in Kenosha, in Vacaville, California, and in Potomac Mills, Virginia. But outlet stores were unexpectedly profitable — a cash business with substantial margins — and the trend quickly moved closer to larger metropolitan areas.

By 1987, Jockey stores were meriting more serious attention, and Rick Hosley, vice president of international operations, was doubling as head of Jockey outlets. Hosley saw the opportunity and made moves to compete on an equal footing with traditional shopping centers. When he opened a new store in Michigan City, Indiana, for example, he designed something beyond the usual outlet look of cement floors and wooden bins. This one was launched with full department-store furniture and polish. Other outlet retailers thought Jockey was overreaching, but the results told the tale, and other apparel manufacturers quickly followed suit.

Ed Emma was hired in 1991 to be Jockey's vice president of the Retail Store Division — a new position reflecting the importance of the stores, not only as a source of revenue, but as an opportunity to promote brand loyalty. Emma and his successor in the retail division, Michael Lapidus, instilled a strong esprit de corps among sales associates. They ended each sale by offering a membership in the Jockey Club, which gave card-carrying members $20 of free merchandise for every $200 spent.

Besides getting repeat business, the Jockey Club helped the company collect hard data on buying habits, which Lapidus saw as basic to doing business in the twenty-first century. "The information that we get from a single sale is as important as the transaction itself," he said. In this case, customer-tracking software was applied along with the age-old objective of creating a connection between the company and its customers.

Retailing Speed and Efficiency

Other trends in retailing called for other innovations. In this period, the old-fashioned personal touch was frankly less important to large department stores, which were buying each other, consolidating and centralizing functions, including their buyers. The trend was obvious by the late 1980s, when Dayton's, the Minneapolis department store, absorbed the Hudson Stores in Detroit, and by 1994 Dayton-Hudson purchased Marshall Field's of Chicago. In the early 1990s, Federated Department Stores, a national chain with longtime strength in the East, moved to California by purchasing Macy's and Broadway stores, and Dillard's of Little Rock bought the Mercantile Stores, itself a chain of once-independent department stores. Dozens of store locations now required a single Jockey salesperson.

The practical effect was that the once-sprawling sales force shrank from 130 in the early 1980s to a streamlined 39 in the

Ed Emma came to Jockey as vice president of retail stores in 1991. When he became president of the company in 1995, he balanced his excitement for new products with the goal of stabilizing Jockey's position in the classic white underwear business.

mid-1990s. These and other changes were managed by Ed Gill, previously a territory salesman and sales manager who became senior vice president of customer logistics. As much as anyone in the company, Gill introduced Jockey's modern selling style, now corporate- and data-driven.

Reorganization meant new kinds of positions, such as inside sales personnel to handle telemarketing and sales associates who took care of the in-store housekeeping chores that traveling salesmen had done previously. These changes were accompanied by the pioneering use of electronic data interchange. Inspired by Jockey's old model stock program, the pride of the industry in the 1950s, the new reordering system used in-store scanning data to monitor stock and order shipments automatically. This began with Dillard's and Dayton-Hudson working with Jockey to set standards and protocols as early as 1986. By the late 1990s, 95 percent

As Jockey underwear keeps a step ahead of fashion, so do the retail stores. In 1979 the store in Orlando, Florida — not yet the South's great tourist mecca — was architecturally ahead of the curve, with quality fixtures and orderly merchandise.

of all of Jockey's domestic reorders were done electronically.

E-Commerce

A later milestone in Jockey sales and marketing was e-commerce, which evolved as management kept its ear to the ground for a clear signal of public needs and preferences. Just as the company's original knitting mill prospered because of Reverend Samuel Cooper's personal contact with customers, modern marketing techniques were focused on the same old-fashioned objective. "Web sites are designed to collect feedback," said Jockey's Webmaster, Chris Smith, when the company

established a site on the World Wide Web in 1998.

E-mails quickly came in with useful information. Many pointed out that they used the internet to find hard-to-get merchandise and cited nylon men's underwear and big-and-tall sizes as the kinds of things they couldn't easily find in retail stores. Customer service maintained a file of thousands of such messages. Then when Jockey launched e-commerce sales in November 2000, each past inquiry was answered with a personal message, and some with a note that nylon boxers, for example, or size 50 Jockey shorts were available through the Internet. This personal touch —

something that Jockey had stressed for all of its 125 years — helped bring loyal customers to this most modern sales channel of all.

Strategic Partnerships Worldwide

While Jockey mastered new ways of selling in America, the company also widened its worldwide influence as well. The Jockey name remained powerful in markets where licensees had been building market share for decades. It was doing very nicely, too, in emerging markets along the Pacific Rim. Then in 1999, with a view to the future lowering of import-export duties negotiated by the World Trade Organization, Jockey based its new president of the international division, Greg Parker, in Australia. A "unified worldwide image" was how Parker described Jockey's international objective at the time.

A unified image meant a similar identity in all of the 120 countries where Jockey was doing business. Uniformity had been behind Jockey's 1997 purchase of British licensee Courtauld Ltd, which had earlier purchased Lyle and Scott, and making the Courtauld operation in Gateshead, England, a central distribution center for most of Europe. Consolidating the European business also meant standardizing the classic white underwear business and eventually the fashion lines as well. "The way for us to grow is to establish a consistent look the world over," said Manoj Chadha, director of the international division.

Uniformity did not mean that every market was treated the same. Jockey fashions continued to reflect local personality. The longtime popularity of the Y-Front design, for example, inspired German licensee, Volma Wirkwaren GmbH, to come out with a line of women's briefs and bras fashioned with Y-Front-like seams. "Ohne Y fehlt dir wars" —"Without the Y something is missing" — was the tag line for a German ad shortly after the new products were introduced in 1998. In 1999, licensee Pacific Dunlop Holdings developed a line of briefs and bras for New Zealand called Jockey Woman. The line was sold in partnership with Farmer's, a major national department store chain, and acquired a 20 percent market share in little more than three months.

Jockey's global presence in the 1990s also

meant manufacturing. Moving swiftly into the changing marketplace, Jockey struck "strategic partnerships" with major concerns, largely in the Far East, which could both manufacture and market Jockey. Such partnerships included a multi-tiered relationship with Daiwabo Textiles, Jockey's Japanese licensee, which also provided textile and sewing capacity in developing countries such as Indonesia.

As Jockey and its sourcing department, created in 1994, did business with many developing countries, a key objective in each case was for Jockey to make a positive contribution to the people who lived there. To reinforce this commitment, the company was one of three U.S. firms to spearhead the Worldwide Responsible Apparel Production group, formed in the year 2000 to establish anti-sweatshop standards. "We're sending a clear message," said Ed Emma when the initiative was presented to officials in Washington and to other companies. "We won't tolerate inhumane conditions in any factories anywhere."

Advertising Fashion

Jockey was blazing new trails at home as well, particularly in the revamped department stores of America, where the rise of designer fashions was making Jockey's once-familiar retail space a fresh battleground. Stalwart brands like Jockey were now sharing department store venues with designers such as

Senior Vice President Ed Gill started as a salesman in Kansas, selling underwear and sportswear in what he liked to call "the leisure suit capital of the nation." When he came to Kenosha, he used his experience to guide the evolution of the sales force, which had to adapt to consolidation in the retail industry and the explosion of information technology.

Calvin Klein, Yves St. Laurent, Ralph Lauren and others, who attracted attention with in-store boutiques, blazing signage and high-fashion lines that included underwear.

High fashion was a complex arena, especially for a company that was still best known for the classic brief. Jockey's response was carefully crafted to promote a fashion-forward image without sacrificing its reputation for comfort. "Let 'Em Known You're Jockey" was the signature of a series of ads launched in 1998 with "real people" in fashion underwear. They were firemen, doctors, surfers and stockbrokers showing off their Jockeys — in most cases with their pants around their ankles. "It was attractive and it had humor," said Debra Steigerwaldt Waller, vice president of marketing and advertising when the campaign was launched. "And best of all it attracted attention."

"Let 'Em Know You're Jockey" coincided with the opening of a new New York sales office in November 1998. For the previous half-century, Jockey had been sold out of the Empire State Building. Now Ed Emma and his staff concluded that a new sales floor in the fashionable precincts of New York's garment district would infuse the company with a younger and more dynamic image. Dynamic it was, and for the opening of the showroom, guests were escorted to the unveiling of Jockey's latest billboard on Times Square. Journalists swarmed when the models in the giant ad, young snowboarders from the Rocky Mountains, appeared live, "dropped trow," and let the world know what kind of underwear they wore when they were "hitting a kicker" on the slopes.

Designers of the Future

There seemed no limit to how fashionable underwear might become. In 1981, for example, Jockey had blazed an altogether new trail with a contract with Yves St. Laurent to make and market briefs, boxers and tee-shirts with the designer's high-fashion trademark. Jockey's YSL underwear had a short run, as did a pair of other licensed brands, Perry Ellis in 1985 and Christian Dior in 1989. Again, some wondered if Jockey's non-Jockey labels might not dilute the power of its own trademark. Yet management moved resolutely back into high-end fashion.

At the end of the 1990s, Jockey had contracts with two of the design industry's biggest names — Tommy Hilfiger and Liz Claiborne. Both agreements demonstrated the company's agility in responding to change. The Tommy Hilfiger relationship came first, and it succeeded nicely for both sides when Jockey people acclimated themselves to the fast-moving and assertive ways of New York fashion.

Then in 1998, the Liz Claiborne license, under which Jockey produced and sold a full line of ladies' undergarments called Liz Claiborne Intimates, moved forward swiftly and smoothly without any hint of culture clash. "Jockey's a preeminent marketer, and they share our values of fit and quality," said Liz Claiborne's president, Paul Charron, shortly after the agreement was signed.

This happy marriage was symbolic of Jockey's ability to adapt, as it had for decades and in many different ways. It was a smooth-flowing two-way street, in fact. The high-fashion contingent from New York had the vision to embrace an old line Wisconsin knitter. For its part, the knitter understood its own strengths well enough to translate them for a world where the basics are positioned firmly and immovably beneath the surface.

The Meaning of Jockey

If Samuel Cooper and his sons reappeared in the year 2000, they would have been mystified, no doubt, by modern underwear — the styles, the fabrics and most of all the advertising. But they quickly would have recognized the ideas behind them. Those ideas address core values established by Jockey's founders and have been a big part of every success story along the way. Clearly, Ed Emma's mission when he became president of the company in 1995 was to focus on the company's core values and to build on them.

That kind of focus was harder than ever at the end of the 1990s, however, with a market

Debra Steigerwaldt Waller, Donna's daughter, had been a teacher before she joined the company to help design and merchandise Jockey for Her. Debra represents one of Jockey's greatest strengths from its beginning—the sense of family that provided stability in an often volatile fashion world. As she rose in the company, Waller has made sure the company adheres to the old strengths of quality, comfort and fit. She became chairman in 2001, after her mother's death.

Jockey in the House?

Let 'em know you're
JOCKEY.

Doctors, Surgeons and Physical Therapists
Los Angeles County
November 15, 1997

The "Let 'Em Know Your Jockey" campaign, left, was original in 1997 when it was introduced, but it also did what Jockey advertising had been doing for years. It challenged social mores without overstepping them. It not only made an impression in magazines and on billboards; it got free publicity as it portrayed in this ad a side of the medical profession that had been hidden far too long.

that was growing, changing and moving at a frenetic pace. To simplify focus, Emma had reorganized the company in 1996, dividing its merchandising and marketing arts into five basic segments — with separate Designer, Retail, International, Thoroughbred (private label) and Jockey Brand Divisions. Each was created to identify its own strengths, track its own results and build its own future. They would interact richly, but the market had already shown that different customers in the marketplace required different approaches.

The largest and arguably most important

of the divisions was Jockey Brand, responsible for the traditional business from the classic styles to the range of fashion-forward products for men and women. With new energy, Jockey Brand president Bob Nolan reaffirmed many important features of the oldest name in underwear. One was that the brand had "elasticity" — it sold to a wide range of consumers, from the price-minded to those shopping in some of America's finest department stores. Another was that what consumers expected above all from Jockey was comfort.

These insights reinforced new efforts in product design and advertising as the company moved toward its 125th anniversary. It meant that Jockey would use only premium cotton henceforward — California combed cotton, primarily because it was softer when new and more durable after wear. It provided comfort for the wearer, both physical and economic, and it had an almost immediate effect on sales.

Jockey advertising also changed to reinforce the comfort message. "The next best thing to naked" was one slogan. Psychological

THE SOFT CUP BRA

JOCKEY® <
THE NEXT BEST THING TO   NAKED.

In 2001, Jockey inaugurated its "Next Best Thing" campaign, left, which featured a series of products, most of them cotton, in modern settings that conveyed a comfortable, unencumbered lifestyle.

comfort was suggested in photography with vintage cars and in locations such as glass houses in wide-open spaces. Images stressed comfort in the full range of products, from stretch-Lycra undershorts, good for the office or sports, to No-Panty Line products that looked great under tighter, formfitting fashions.

Success in these campaigns proved that comfort was the key and any way to transmit that message, through subtle or unsubtle means, was part of the brand-building process. Success also reinforced the lesson

that while some things were fluid and changed with every passing season, the core values stood rock solid. As a practical matter, understanding core values made it possible to lead the way in imaginative design — several new products made Jockey the fashion leader in 2001 — but also benefit from the ages-old promise of quality, comfort and fit.

Beyond its new lines and designs, the modern Jockey was rethinking what it meant to be not just a trademark but a brand — the sum and substance of expectations and aspirations. "Advertising reaches into the

mind," says Nolan. "Branding reaches into the heart." There aren't many trademarks in the apparel business that express quite as much as Jockey does. Success depends upon the company protecting this asset and building on it.

"We're blessed with a strong image, for fit, for quality and for comfort," says Emma. "Beyond all that, Jockey's known for innovation. It means we have to work to keep those core values strong. The spirit of Jockey is a gift, and this gift also comes with a responsibility to keep up with the public's expectations."

Epilogue

Since becoming chairman of Jockey in 2001, I have been increasingly convinced that Jockey's continued success depends on its ability to learn from its past. Nostalgic sentimentality simply is not enough. We must be able to translate our legacy into timely strategies that perpetuate and build on our rich heritage.

This has never been easy for any company. Many brands, driven by economic jitters and unnerving changes in the marketplace, have self-destructed by misunderstanding or ignoring their heritage. They have forgotten the substance of their history and developed the marketing equivalent of a multiple personality disorder in frantic efforts to find their way.

For most of its 125 years, Jockey has avoided this trap by understanding its foundations. In an industry increasingly populated by newcomers, Jockey has managed to maintain its own clear identity and appeal to consumers. It has achieved this largely by understanding its history and core values.

At the same time, Jockey must also avoid sacrificing its future on the altar of history. As we have seen, some companies have been too much enamored with the glories of their past. Those organizations have refused to change with the times, ultimately failing to learn a cardinal lesson of history: greatness is always a by-product of change.

History is a guide, not a straitjacket.

While continuing to nurture Jockey's distinctive identity in department stores, for example, we must also acknowledge change in that channel, as evidenced by the recent growth of designer brands. In response to this trend, Jockey has aggressively secured designer licenses in order to compete successfully in this arena. We must continue to be sensitive to change and to opportunity — always looking for the chance to extend our heritage of quality, comfort and innovation. Change within the context of tradition applies to other distribution channels whose growth warrants the introduction of Jockey-owned brands, such as Formfit and Life, which have been developed for the growing mass merchandising retail chains.

As the twenty-first century promises to be one of unprecedented technological change, Jockey is taking a lead in reversing our industry's reluctance to adopt new ways of doing things. Jockey is investing in a variety of cutting-edge initiatives, as it has already done with electronic data interchange (EDI) and JBA, our groundbreaking IT networking system. Now on the table is the growth and value of the Internet, a tool that represents unlimited promise in improving our external and internal operations. Moreover, our move into modern new quarters in Kenosha County will represent another aspect of modernizing without compromising our strengths. While Jockey must not lag behind, neither can the company afford a reckless race for newness for its own sake, which can easily result in losses on the scale of the "dot-com" debacle at the turn of the twenty-first century.

Ultimately, Jockey's future depends on balance. We must value our past without being restricted by it. We must foster our business in successful, tried-and-true distribution channels without turning a blind eye to the potential of new ones. We must invest in technology without squandering our assets on technological novelties. We must nurture our own distinct brands without overlooking opportunities for partnerships with other brands. In essence, Jockey must change with the times — and yet remain Jockey.

As chairman, I have never been more convinced that our continued progress depends entirely upon our employees. Principles and values are only as good as the people who put them into practice. This was the most important lesson of my mother, who preceded me in this office. Donna Wolf Steigerwaldt always recognized that Jockey's people are its number-one reason for success. They always have been and they always will be. Our future rests in their hands, just as it has for 125 years.

Debra S. Waller

Debra Steigerwaldt Waller
Chairman and CEO

Acknowledgments

Reconstructing 125 years of Jockey history was a pleasure for many reasons, and one of them was that it enabled me to reconstruct a part of my own childhood. My late father, Joseph W. Pridmore, was a Jockey vice president for two years in the early 1960s, and some of my earliest memories of his working career were of the impressive people he worked for, including Harry Wolf Sr., Robert Cooper and Hal Sommer.

Beyond that personal note, the cooperation of many people was essential to the research and writing of this book. Among them, Chairman and CEO Debra Steigerwaldt Waller, President and COO Ed Emma and Senior Vice President Ed Gill provided support and structure to this book.

As a primary source of historical information, the Jockey International archive in Kenosha contains the company's most complete record of letters, clippings, newsletters, photos and other material. Jockey archivist/corporate communications manager John Cronce was a patient and essential resource from beginning to end.

Many people were interviewed for this history, including retirees and former employees Jim Andreucci, Howard Cooley, Bill Hermann, Fred Holmes, Rick Hosley, Shirley Jackson, Mac Millholland, Howie Ness, Ernie Ott, Carl Radke, Jim Roach, Paul Sebastian, Wayne Shumate and Hal Sommer.

Also interviewed were current employees Joe Burke, Manoj Chadha, Peter Hannes, Ken Houston, Mike Lapidus, Mike Jablecki, Vicki Kalcic, Charlie Lamb, Marty Mankowski, Bob Nolan, Helen Reetz, Al Rennett, Don Ruland and Hanie Yee. Betty Moseley was helpful in identifying people to interview and arranging those interviews. Noreen Wilkinson and Mandy Bergeson also assisted in locating various resources that were important in bringing *There's Only One* to completion.

Jockey's New York publicist Erica Feinberg and Arthur Kneibler's daughter Mary Kneibler were generous with their time and memories, and they helped give this book dimensions that it otherwise would not have. Mac Millholland's wife, Sis, was also willing and eager to help with the story of her father, Gilbert S. Lance.

Other resources that were used in *There's Only One* were the *Kenosha News*, the Kenosha Historical Society, the Berrien County Historical Society in Michigan, the Simmons Library in Kenosha and the St. Joseph Public Library in Michigan. Those institutions and their librarians were more than generous in providing documents that added, in some cases, wonderful details in the telling of the Jockey story. To all these people, I offer my sincere thanks and the hope that this history is worthy of their kind contributions.

Jay Pridmore
May 2001

Timeline

1876
S. T. Cooper & Sons, manufacturer of wool hosiery and predecessor of Jockey International, Inc., is founded in St. Joseph, Michigan.

1878
Michigan businessman Abel Wells invests money to build a knitting mill for the young company. The company is renamed Cooper, Wells & Co. and the mill is known as the Industrial Knitting Mill.

1892
Founder Samuel T. Cooper dies, and his sons Willis and Charles leave Cooper, Wells & Company to invest in and help run a new Kenosha, Wisconsin, factory for the Chicago-Rockford Hosiery Company, the maker of Black Cat hosiery, later renamed Chicago-Kenosha Hosiery Company.

1900
Brothers Willis, Henry and Charles Cooper incorporate Cooper Underwear Company in Kenosha. The company manufactures White Cat union suits in a corner of the Black Cat mill.

1902
A new mill for the manufacture of White Cat union suits is completed next door to the Black Cat mill. This location on 60th Street later becomes the longtime headquarters of Jockey International.

1903
The infamous Iroquois Theater fire in Chicago claims the lives of Willis and Charles Cooper. Henry Cooper becomes the sole head of Cooper Underwear.

1909
Henry Cooper and plant superintendent Horace Greeley Johnson create the closed crotch union suit, a state of the art design that becomes the standard for comfort and quality construction in men's underwear.

1912
The Cooper union suit is branded as the Kenosha Klosed Krotch. Henry Cooper hires Joseph Leyendecker to create a print ad for this union suit. The resulting illustration, known as the "Man on the Bag" remains one of advertising's most famous images. Also this year, Cooper Underwear separates completely from Black Cat/Allen-A Hosiery.

1918
Cooper Underwear opens a new plant in Manistee, Michigan, to increase production capacity during World War I. But the armistice in November would mean an oversupply in the textile industry and hard times for Cooper Underwear.

1921
Cooper Underwear enters the hosiery market, introducing hosiery for men, women and children.

1922
Tips and Pointer for Underwear Dealers and Their Salesman, one of the most detailed sales manuals of the era, is published by Cooper Underwear.

1924
Henry Cooper dies, and his son Robert Cooper takes over as president.

1928
Arthur Kneibler joins Cooper Underwear as vice president of sales.

1929
Cooper Underwear Company, long known as "Coopers" changes its official name to Coopers, Inc., reflecting more diverse product offerings.

1930
Ralph Cooper, the late Henry's nephew, assumes control of the company from Robert. Gilbert S. Lance, Ralph Cooper's brother-in-law, invests substantially in the company and becomes corporate secretary. Harry Wolf Sr. becomes an independent auditor of Coopers, beginning a relationship with the company that he would one day own.

1934
Art Kneibler devises the pioneering Jockey short, the first example of what is known today as the classic brief.

1935
The Y-Front design becomes an indispensable feature of Jockey shorts, enhancing the "masculinized support" function of the product.

1936
Coopers becomes the first to use individual cellophane packaging for underwear, helping move it out of the back room and up to the front of the store displays.

1937
Coopers creates the "stride form" mannequin to supply stores with a display that will properly show the fit and function of Jockey underwear.

1938
Coopers features a "Cellophane Wedding," at its annual sales convention, calling attention to the unique Jockey design and its individual cellophane packaging and capturing international publicity for Jockey underwear. Also that year, an Australian licensee, MacRae Knitting Mills, is contracted to make and sell Jockey products in Australia.

1939
A Jockey salesman invents a countertop dispenser to organize sizes and styles of Jockey underwear.

1940
To protect the Jockey brand name, Coopers commissions the Jockey Boy trademark and icon, introduced at the annual sales convention.

1942
Vollmoeller Knitting Works is licensed to make and sell Jockey in Switzerland. This company later helps develop new markets and licensees throughout Europe after World War II.

1947
The Jockey name is stitched into the waistband of underwear for the first time.

1948
Coopers first works with Kentucky contract manufacturer, Giffin Manufacturing, which later becomes Blue Grass Industries.

1951
Coopers expands its operations to Millen, Georgia, its first plant in the Deep South.

1954
Coopers advertises in the first issue of *Sports Illustrated*.

1958
Coopers introduces Jockey Skants, the company's first foray into mass-market fashion underwear. Coopers also purchases its first TV advertising. The humorous spot, read by Jack Parr on the *Tonight Show* looks at first glance like a debacle, but becomes a popular ad.

1960
Gilbert S. "Gib" Lance dies. Harry Wolf acquires Coopers stock from his widow, Carlotta Cooper Lance, assuming majority control and chairmanship of Coopers.

1964
Harry Wolf Sr. acquires control of manufacturer Blue Grass Industries.

1965
Coopers introduces Jockey Life as a full line of fashion underwear in varied colors.

1971
Coopers, Inc., changes its official name to Jockey Menswear. Jack Wyss becomes president of the company.

1972
The company name changes again to Jockey International, Inc.

1975
Jack Wyss retires from the presidency and is replaced by Dick Jensen.

1976
Harry Wolf Sr. retires from the chairmanship and is replaced by his son, Harry Wolf Jr., known as "Buddy." The introduction of the Jockey Elance line of bikini style briefs begins the company's long leadership in fashion underwear for men. Jim Palmer makes his first appearance in a Jockey advertisement, beginning a relationship with the company that would grow into one of the most famous ad campaigns of the 1970s and 1980s.

1978
Donna Wolf Steigerwaldt becomes chairman and CEO the company. Jockey opens its first outlet store, in Kenosha, Wisconsin.

1979
Consultant Howard Cooley is hired on as president.

1981
Jockey acquires its first designer license and establishes a line of men's underwear for Yves St. Laurent.

1982
The introduction of Jockey For Her makes the most famous name in men's underwear also the most comfortable name in women's underwear.

1987
Jockey opens its first offshore manufacturing facility in Lucea, Jamaica.

1993
Jockey begins a licensing agreement to produce underwear for Tommy Hilfiger.

1995
Edward C. Emma, formerly head of Jockey outlet stores, is named Jockey's president and COO.

1996
Jockey establishes Thorobred Brands to consolidate its "other-name" business in discount chains and other markets outside traditional venue of department stores and menswear stores.

1997
Jockey buys British licensee Courtauld Ltd as part of an effort to consolidate European operations. The 100th Jockey store opens.

1998
The Jockey Web site debuts. Jockey's licensing agreement with Liz Claiborne brings Jockey style and comfort to designer lingerie.

1999
Jockey introduces its first line of bras.

2000
Donna Steigerwaldt dies after more than 12 years at the helm of Jockey International.

2001
Debra Steigerwaldt Waller succeeds her mother as the new chairman and CEO of Jockey International. The company celebrates 125 years since the establishment of S. T. Cooper & Sons.

Index

Page numbers appear in boldface for illustrations.